Transform
Your Teaching
With **Universal Design**
for **Learning**

Transform
Your Teaching
With **Universal Design** for **Learning**

Six Steps to Jumpstart Your Practice

Jennifer L. Pusateri

CAST | Until learning has no limits*

Library of Congress Control Number: 2022940137

Paperback ISBN 978-1-930583-95-5
Ebook ISBN 978-1-930583-94-8

Published by:
CAST Professional Publishing
an imprint of CAST, Inc.
Wakefield, Massachusetts, USA

Cover design, interior design, and production by Happenstance Type-O-Rama

For bulk discounts and other inquiries, email publishing@cast.org or visit
www.castpublishing.org.

To Sister Anne Rita Mauck,
who dared to believe
in her students

Contents

Introduction

Why Write This Book?

I come from a long line of educators. Both my parents are retired teachers, my grandmother was a teacher, and my great-grandfather taught in a one-room schoolhouse in southern Illinois in the early 1900s (see Figure 1). I feel pretty confident in my ability to speak and understand the language of teachers and have made it a point in my career to help teachers design

FIGURE 1. My great-grandfather, Arnot McArthy, and his students, standing in front of a one-room schoolhouse in Southern Illinois; photo taken around 1917 or 1918.

innovative lessons that will engage all kinds of students. When I was in the classroom, I taught arts and humanities at a school for students with specific learning disabilities (SLD), and approximately 80% of my students either had a diagnosis for or displayed symptoms consistent with ADHD. My administrators didn't want me to give students grades, so I had to rely entirely on my ability to design engaging lessons that took into account the many learning barriers that accompany learning disabilities. I quickly learned that in order for my students to be successful, I would need to find ways to remove distractions, provide scaffolding and supports, and represent information in multiple ways. I saw the brilliance in my students emerge because I was proactively anticipating and removing learning barriers before they became a problem. I wouldn't know until several years later, but teaching at that school was my accidental introduction to Universal Design for Learning (UDL).

At the time, I gave an assignment to one of my third-grade classes in which I asked them to create a newspaper to demonstrate their understanding of the concepts they had just learned during a science unit on the ocean. When I showed the school administrators the final product, they asked me why I decided to do a project like this. My answer was "When I planned this activity, I was thinking about Sam—a student who is very intelligent but who shuts down when asked to write more than a few words. I knew Sam probably wouldn't be able to express what he'd actually learned if he was given a paper-and-pencil test. But because I've seen Sam's artwork in my art class, I know that he is an exceptional cartoonist. So, I tried to think of a way that Sam could show what he'd learned in a different way, possibly with a comic strip or a cartoon. Then I started thinking of other students in the class and what options I could give them to show what they'd learned. The result? I decided the assignment should be a newspaper because that would allow students multiple ways to demonstrate understanding (comics, articles, advertisements, opinion pieces, photography, etc.)."

One of my administrators said, "Hang on. Have you heard of Universal Design for Learning? You should check it out!"

Unfortunately, it would be several more years before I discovered that I had been accidentally doing UDL the whole time I was teaching!

Now, some UDLers may balk at this idea of accidental UDL because they may believe that you can't do UDL without knowing that you're doing UDL. And although I understand my colleagues' concerns with using this terminology, I think it *is* possible to be doing things in your classroom that align with UDL ideas (proactively designing instruction that attempts to reduce learning barriers for all learners) without actually having seen the UDL framework. Indeed, after studying UDL in earnest for the last six years, I know for certain that I was "doing UDL" before, but I was unaware that there was a name for what I was doing.

In 2016 I attended the second annual CAST UDL Symposium at Harvard and found myself nodding in agreement in almost every session I attended. It was as if a switch was flipped for me over the course of a three-day conference. What had really happened? I had shifted my mindset. My perspective changed from believing that the problems I saw in my classroom were because of my students to one in which I fully understood that many of the problems I saw were because of the curriculum's design. This mindset shift was subtle, but extremely powerful. You see, if the problem is with the students, a teacher can't do much to fix it. However, if I believe that the problem isn't with the students, but rather with the way I've designed the learning environment and activities . . . now, that's something I can work with!

Over the last six years I've immersed myself in UDL because I've seen the transformative power of proactively planning for the inevitable, a classroom filled with diverse learners, and now I want all teachers to know that they, too, can learn how UDL can shift their thinking about teaching and learning. Indeed, I've made it my mission to make UDL accessible to teachers by giving them some concrete ways to design lessons and instruction with the UDL framework.

In my professional roles at the Kentucky Department of Education and the University of Kentucky's Center for the Enhancement of Learning and Teaching (CELT), and as a CAST National Faculty presenter, I've given trainings, workshops, and conference sessions about UDL to thousands of educators in K–12 and higher education settings all over the U.S. One of the most common questions I receive comes from educators who ask me to how to "do UDL." Most of the time, I know these teachers understand and agree with the theory or ideas behind UDL, but they get stuck when it comes to implementing UDL. I totally understand where they are coming from since six years ago, I was also a new UDL convert, energized by how this flexible framework offers a way to reach all learners, regardless of their backgrounds, learning differences, age, or grade level. I knew UDL was the bomb, but it wasn't immediately clear how to apply it. I needed a systematic way to understand how to use this color-coded grid that was filled with research-heavy language and bullet points. I needed to change the way I taught, but I wasn't finding many step-by-step examples that broke this process down for me. In my case, I had developed a UDL mindset, but I didn't have the tools to put my new mindset into practice.

It wasn't until I was asked to lead a workshop on lesson planning with UDL that I sat down and thought through a way to operationalize the two factors I find are necessary to become comfortable designing instruction with UDL: 1) shifting your theoretical mindset and 2) employing practical design approaches and UDL-aligned strategies. While preparing for this workshop, I was reminded of a UDL and Design Thinking session I attended at the 2016 CAST UDL Symposium. Session leader Kim Ducharme (CAST's UX design director) walked us through the world of journey mapping and used it to modify an existing lesson plan. I *loved* the experience of looking at each segment of the lesson through the student's eyes and using that perspective to search for potential barriers to learning in the lesson, as well as in the materials, environment, and methods. Journey mapping a lesson plan offered me a great way to visualize how to plan lessons, but I was concerned that the format might be a little too complicated for a UDL newbie who wanted to dig in and implement UDL right away. I was determined to find another way to help teachers become comfortable with UDL so they could plan and modify lessons easily.

In my experience introducing UDL to educators across the U.S., I have found that most teachers don't just jump into UDL like I did. In some cases, getting to a place where you can understand and confidently plan lessons with UDL takes time. It's a process . . . a journey. But I firmly believe that there is a certain period in a teacher's UDL development in which it is crucial that they find practical, operationalized ways to use the UDL Guidelines in designing instruction; if they don't, they may turn their back on UDL and revert to their old ways premised on one-size-fits-all teaching.

These different periods of UDL development remind me of the UDL Progression Rubric designed by Katie Novak and Kristan Rodriguez (2018) that helps teachers determine the degree to which they are implementing UDL in their classrooms. It does this by giving examples of instructional decisions made by teachers who are emerging, proficient, and progressing toward expert practice in their use of UDL (see Figure 2).

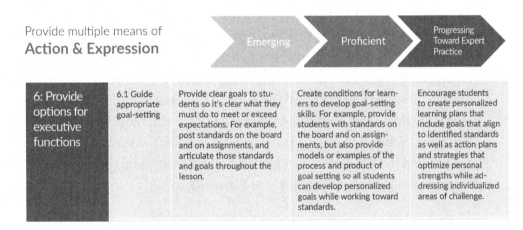

FIGURE 2. An excerpt from the UDL Progression Rubric by Katie Novak and Kristan Rodriguez. © 2022. Novak Education. Used with permission.

This rubric works really well for teachers who are committed to using UDL for planning instruction. But I thought, some teachers new to UDL may not even be at the emerging stage of development. For such teachers, we may need to expand Novak and Rodriguez's rubric to include a larger range of development for how teachers begin to understand and implement UDL into their practice. So, I put pencil to paper and added three more stages or periods that can lead up to the level of an emerging UDL teacher. This is what allowed me to develop the UDL Teacher Development Continuum.

The three new levels that I added to Novak and Rodriguez's UDL Progression Rubric are 1) skeptical, 2) cautiously hopeful, and 3) exploratory. A skeptical teacher understands the concept of UDL but may feel either that UDL is not necessary or that it will not work for them. At this stage, it's not impossible, but it can be difficult to convince such teachers of the power of UDL. Teachers reach the next level of teacher development in UDL when they become cautiously hopeful about the idea of using UDL in their classrooms. They see hope in the idea of instruction that is designed to meet the needs of the variety of students in their room, but they aren't quite ready to make major changes to their classroom or their teaching. Finally, in the last of the three new levels, the exploratory teacher may try making one small change in their instruction, but this stage is fraught because if they run into problems or snags during this trial run, they may give up on UDL.

This critical period occurs between the levels of cautiously hopeful and emergent. I've found that if we don't support teachers in this critical period of UDL development with concrete, practical ways to build UDL into their teaching, they may become overwhelmed and abandon UDL altogether. The goal of this book is to provide UDL newbies with three graduated approaches to UDL lesson design that will help get them through the critical period of UDL development (see Figure 3).

The UDL Teacher Development Continuum

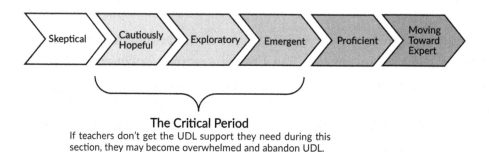

The Critical Period
If teachers don't get the UDL support they need during this section, they may become overwhelmed and abandon UDL.

FIGURE 3. This book will help teachers through the critical period.

The lesson planning approaches, strategies, graphic organizers, planning templates, techniques, and tips in this book serve as a blueprint to help novice UDL teachers gain confidence in using the UDL framework and offer them tools to design and implement teaching and learning experiences that support all learners.

Who Is This Book For?

Integrating UDL into your practice typically involves a critical shift in how you think about teaching; this shift asks you to anticipate and plan for how to get around potential barriers that learners may encounter in any given situation. UDL also asks teachers to keep these potential barriers in mind as they think about their curricular goals, methods, materials, and assessments and how they may need to adapt these elements of their curriculum.

This mindset shift can take place quickly or slowly, but it is absolutely essential that you go through this shift in order to begin your own UDL journey. For some educators this shift from the one-size-fits-all classrooms that many of us grew up in is a huge leap. For others, the idea of proactively designing instruction based on the variety of students in their classrooms is fundamental to the work that they do every day, and learning about UDL reinforces the truths they've always felt in their teacher soul. But for teachers who are new to UDL, this mindset shift may have yet to take place. Others may have a general understanding of UDL but not see it as necessary or relevant to their classroom. This book is designed to help educators develop or strengthen their UDL mindset and to equip them with planning approaches and strategies to help them move confidently on their path to long-lasting UDL implementation.

Regardless of where you are in your UDL journey, you've come to the right place!

Most narrowly, *Transform Your Teaching With Universal Design for Learning* is a workbook written for K–8 educators, administrators, paraprofessionals, instructional coaches, and teacher-leaders who already have a general understanding of UDL and are looking for practical ways to use UDL in their classrooms. However, if this is the first you've heard of UDL—for instance, someone in a professional learning community (PLC) handed you this book and you've had no prior introduction—you may want to consider reading a book that introduces the basic concepts, like Katie Novak's *UDL Now! A Teacher's Guide to Applying Universal Design for Learning* (2022) or *Universal Design for Learning: Theory and Practice* (2014) by Anne Meyer, David H. Rose, and David Gordon, before diving into this book.

Parts 1 and 2 of the book offer you a six-step roadmap that guides you through how to think about UDL and then integrate its framework so that it begins to be second nature. The process of developing a UDL mindset begins with questions to help you develop or strengthen your UDL mindset. These questions are accompanied by specific exercises that will help you move through the process. You can move through these six steps at whatever pace works best for you. The emphasis of this text for the UDL practitioner is always to be intentional and proactive in planning for the needs of all individual learners rather than merely being reactive (as, for example, differentiated instruction is).

What Is in This Book?

This book is divided into three main parts. Part 1 takes you through the first four steps of a six-step process to develop or strengthen your UDL mindset. In part 2, you are introduced to the next two steps, including descriptions of how three different approaches to lesson design can be used to implement UDL. The Plus-One approach, the Troubleshooting approach, and the Journey-Mapping approach offer you three options for integrating or "trying on" UDL, with specific tips on how to consider goals, predict learning barriers, and design (or redesign) lessons to remove those barriers. Part 2 also offers a quick review of the UDL principles and guidelines and suggestions on how to easily begin to exercise your new UDL mindset. Finally, part 3 offers a collection of accessible teaching strategies that show you how to apply UDL's Guidelines and checkpoints. (Expanded and printable versions of some of these UDL-aligned teaching strategies can be found on the *tinyurl.com/TransformWithUDL* website.)

It's important to note here that there is no such thing as a UDL strategy. UDL is not a set of strategies or techniques. It is a framework that helps teachers plan instruction that removes learning barriers for students. Countless strategies can do this. In fact, teachers are probably already employing some strategies and techniques in their current instruction that align with the ideas of UDL. However, proactively building these strategies in during the planning phase, specifically for the purpose of removing learning barriers, is what UDL is all about!

How to Use This Book

Full disclosure: I typically ignore the introductions and forewords when I read books and skip ahead to Chapter 1. But now that I've written a book, I totally understand why the forewords and introductions are important: They help make the author's intentions and hopes explicit to the reader. How very UDL! So, although you're totally welcome to read this book in the order that makes the most sense to you, the following paragraphs will help you to understand my thinking behind the organization of the various parts and chapters within this book and my hopes for how you will approach it as a reader.

Read

Part 1 guides you through the first four steps of shifting into a UDL mindset. Again, this process enables you to internalize and know UDL in a way that then enables you to integrate UDL into your practice easily. Each step contains exercises and reflective questions to guide you on your way to developing or strengthening your UDL mindset. The second part of the book includes three graduated strategies for planning lessons with UDL. These strategies allow you to move from the simplest, most accessible lesson design approach (the Plus-One approach [Tobin & Behling, 2018]) to a slightly more complex design approach (the Troubleshooting approach) before finishing up with the most complex, but possibly the most impactful approach (the Journey-Mapping approach). If you are newer to UDL, this order may work best for you. If you are familiar with UDL and feel comfortable building it into your teaching, feel free to move through the lesson design approaches in whatever order makes the most sense to you. The book ends with part 3 and offers a collection of UDL-aligned strategies that you can use right away!

This book is designed to be an instructional planning handbook that is useful enough to occupy a place of prominence on a teacher's desk. This isn't a shelf book; it's a desk book. By this I mean that educators can return to this book many times rather than just reading it once and putting it on their bookshelf. The templates, lesson-planning approaches, and UDL-aligned strategies make this book a go-to manual when you are planning instruction and solving problems of practice in the classroom.

Annotate

When I was a younger professional, I used to try to keep my books as pristine as possible, thinking I might need to loan them to someone in the future. But over the last decade or so, I've come to realize that reading works best for me when I can annotate a text. I am constantly highlighting, making notes to myself, and drawing pictures to illustrate points in the margins (see Figure 4). It is for this reason that I have intentionally left a good amount of white space around the outside of each page of this book so educators can add notes and draw diagrams and doodle as they read and process the text. Please use this white space to enhance your learning by making connections, posing questions, and marking sections you want to make sure you can find later.

Copy

As mentioned, I've included three different lesson design approaches you can use to try UDL; each comes with a different planning template to help you visualize and organize your thoughts. In Chapter 5, you will find a blank

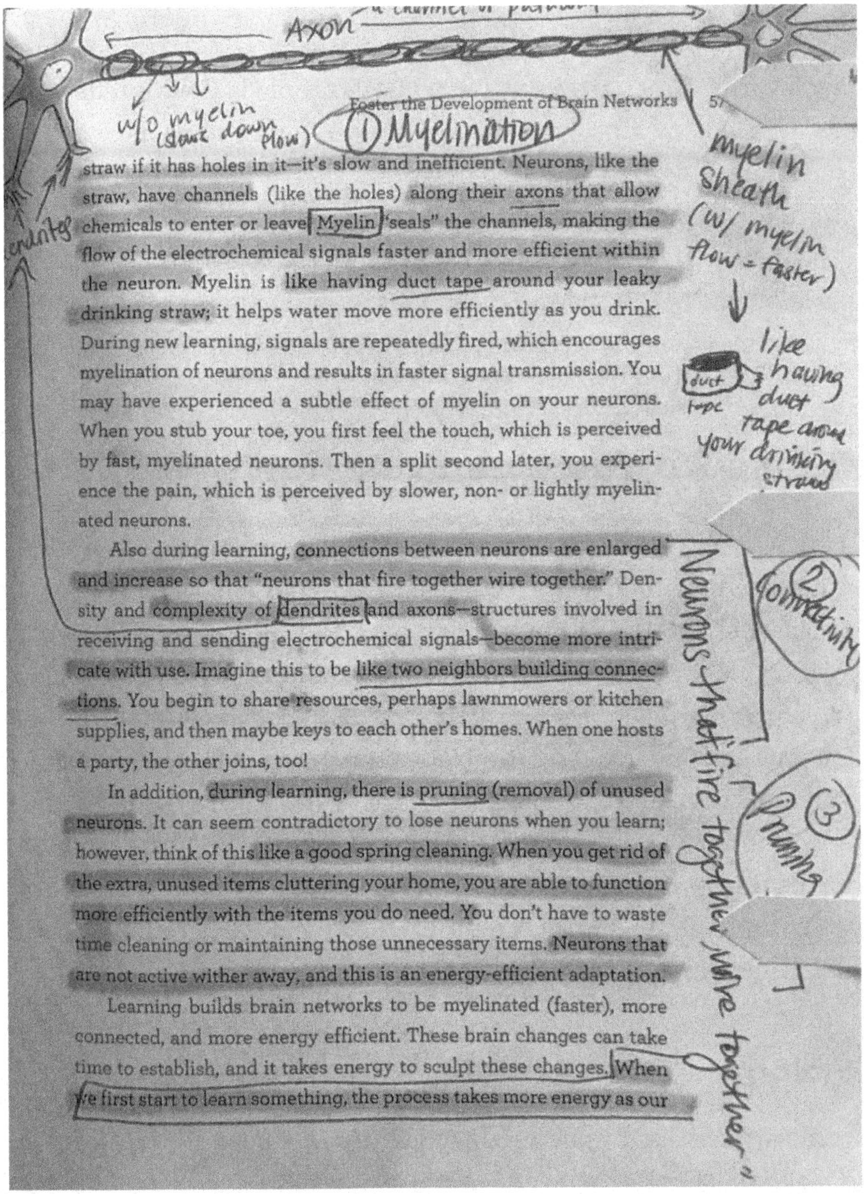

Foster the Development of Brain Networks 57

straw if it has holes in it—it's slow and inefficient. Neurons, like the straw, have channels (like the holes) along their axons that allow chemicals to enter or leave. Myelin "seals" the channels, making the flow of the electrochemical signals faster and more efficient within the neuron. Myelin is like having duct tape around your leaky drinking straw; it helps water move more efficiently as you drink. During new learning, signals are repeatedly fired, which encourages myelination of neurons and results in faster signal transmission. You may have experienced a subtle effect of myelin on your neurons. When you stub your toe, you first feel the touch, which is perceived by fast, myelinated neurons. Then a split second later, you experience the pain, which is perceived by slower, non- or lightly myelinated neurons.

Also during learning, connections between neurons are enlarged and increase so that "neurons that fire together wire together." Density and complexity of dendrites and axons—structures involved in receiving and sending electrochemical signals—become more intricate with use. Imagine this to be like two neighbors building connections. You begin to share resources, perhaps lawnmowers or kitchen supplies, and then maybe keys to each other's homes. When one hosts a party, the other joins, too!

In addition, during learning, there is pruning (removal) of unused neurons. It can seem contradictory to lose neurons when you learn; however, think of this like a good spring cleaning. When you get rid of the extra, unused items cluttering your home, you are able to function more efficiently with the items you do need. You don't have to waste time cleaning or maintaining those unnecessary items. Neurons that are not active wither away, and this is an energy-efficient adaptation.

Learning builds brain networks to be myelinated (faster), more connected, and more energy efficient. These brain changes can take time to establish, and it takes energy to sculpt these changes. When we first start to learn something, the process takes more energy as our

FIGURE 4. Annotations in one of my favorite books, *Engage the Brain*, by Allison Posey (2019)

version of each of the three templates. Please feel free to copy these templates and use them as needed. You can also find printable versions on the *tinyurl.com/TransformWithUDL* website.

Share

One of my favorite things about my fellow UDL people is their intellectual generosity. UDL folks aren't typically too worried about someone stealing their ideas. Most of us are interested in getting UDL out there and spreading the word about its evidence-based practices and theoretical concepts. It is for this reason that I encourage you to share the ideas, strategies, and approaches you find here with your colleagues. If you share your thoughts on Twitter, please tag *@jen_pusateri* and use the hashtag *#TransformWithUDL*.

What Else Do You Need to Know?

I am a person who gets easily confused when reading websites or documents that use terminology in a way that is new to me. In fact, when I first learned about UDL, I didn't understand the difference between a framework, a guideline, a principle, and a checkpoint. Luckily, I stumbled across the book *Design and Deliver: Planning and Teaching Using Universal Design for Learning* by Loui Lord Nelson (2014), which did a fantastic job of explaining the difference between these terms. After that, I was able to better understand the other UDL literature I was reading because Loui had taken the time to *clarify vocabulary and symbols* (UDL checkpoint 2.1). This section will help to clarify the terminology and background knowledge you will encounter throughout this book.

Terminology

Some words are destined to be used frequently in a book like this. In an effort to make this book as conversational as possible, and to avoid using the same terms over and over, I have used some words interchangeably:

- ★ **Teacher/Educator**—Someone who teaches students in a K–8 setting
- ★ **Teaching/Instruction**—The practice of designing and delivering content or skills to students

Grammar and Language

The use of grammar, syntax, and structure in this book is meant to be conversational. As a result, I may switch abruptly from first person to third person, before moving back to second person. This style reflects the way my mind processes information and is the style I use in presentations, workshops, and webinars.

I also use several idioms, or figures of speech, throughout the book. But since these terms and phrases are specific to my language, region, and culture, I will follow them with a secondary explanation of their general meaning.

Grades, School Levels, and Ages

The grades, school levels, and ages of students referred to in this book are based on the United States model of education, which splits students into several levels by age: preschool, elementary school, middle school, high school, and postsecondary. Unfortunately, the division of students into these levels isn't the same across the entire country. In the U.S., most education decisions are made at the state and local level, as opposed to being federally (or nationally) mandated, so one model does not fit all U.S. schools. Table 1 is meant to clarify the ages, grades, and school levels used in this book so readers can convert the grades, ages, and levels provided into the ones that fit most closely with their system.

TABLE 1. How U.S. Education Is Typically Organized

SCHOOL LEVEL	GRADE	AGES IN YEARS	OTHER NAMES
Elementary	Kindergarten	5–6	Primary
	First grade	6–7	Primary
	Second grade	7–8	Primary
	Third grade	8–9	Primary/Intermediate
	Fourth grade	9–10	Intermediate
	Fifth grade	10–11	Intermediate

TABLE 1 (continued).

SCHOOL LEVEL	GRADE	AGES IN YEARS	OTHER NAMES
Middle	Sixth grade	11–12	Jr. High
	Seventh grade	12–13	Jr. High
	Eighth grade	13–14	Jr. High

Getting in Shape With UDL

Every January, exercise gyms and weight loss programs see a sudden surge when it's time for people to make good on their New Year's resolutions. They look back on the previous year and decide to change something they didn't like, thus hoping to improve their lives in the current year. Some common New Year's resolutions are getting in shape, saving money, paying off debt, and quitting smoking. But despite setting these optimistic goals in early January, most people give them up within a few weeks.

Perhaps the most common New Year's resolution is to get in shape, which can mean different things to different people. For some it may mean losing fat, for others it means building muscle, and for yet others getting in shape can mean building endurance. But regardless of what this means to an individual, the odds are that the process of improving your fitness won't happen overnight. Getting in shape can take weeks, months, years, or even decades. Those who want to get in shape, and more importantly, stay in shape, often find more success when they make small changes gradually rather than trying to change their exercise routine, their eating habits, their caffeine intake, their sleep schedule, and their stress level all at once.

Similarly, deepening your understanding and use of UDL takes time; it, too, is a process, and it's often more sustainable when you implement the changes gradually and intentionally. Planning instruction with the UDL framework is a shift in the way you think about your teaching, and that kind of paradigm shift won't take place over a two-hour professional development workshop or by watching an "Intro to UDL" video. So, as you read this book, and as you continue to learn more about UDL, I encourage you to give yourself time to let the ideas sink in so that you can practice the ideas as you teach, reflect, and consider feedback from your students and begin to integrate the UDL framework and plan your teaching. Slow down, enjoy the process, and try to savor each moment along your UDL journey.

Part 1

Shifting to a UDL Mindset

n the many UDL workshops, webinars, keynotes, and presentations I've taken part in, I've noticed an interesting phenomenon. Some educators have an obvious change in mindset during these sessions and some do not. The teachers who have a major mindset change will, for example, come back on day 2 of a two-day training saying things like, "I couldn't stop thinking about UDL all night. It's like I've started looking for the barriers everywhere!" These educators have often undergone a shift in the way they've always thought about teaching from one where they taught to the average and took care of the struggling and advanced students if they had time to a new way of teaching where they proactively design for the variety of needs in their classroom. I like to call this shift in thinking a *UDL mindset shift*.

This shift often begins with a teacher thinking about how the design of their instruction may have had unintended consequences for their students; the shift continues when these educators think about how they can change their design to help remove these learning barriers for, and with, their students. This mindset shift can take place quickly or slowly, but it is absolutely essential if a teacher wants to begin a UDL journey. In fact, it seems like there are actually two pieces to a teacher finding success with UDL in their classroom: one is the UDL mindset shift and the other is having lesson-planning methods in place that help teachers make these changes to their instruction. If one of these two things is missing (the UDL mindset or the methods to make it happen), implementation of UDL is simply not likely to happen.

> *If teachers have the UDL* mindset, *but don't have a good* method *for planning lessons using the UDL framework, they often get frustrated and give up.*
>
> or
>
> *If teachers have a good lesson-planning* method *for UDL, but they haven't had a shift to a UDL* mindset, *they often see UDL as just another initiative and they give up.*

This book is set up in a series of six steps that move educators through the process of developing a UDL mindset and obtaining some methods for planning UDL instruction. This first part takes you through the first four steps toward developing a UDL mindset. Steps 5 and 6 will be included in the second part of the book, which introduces three methods (called *approaches*) to lesson plan design and several instructional strategies to help you start using UDL in your classroom.

These first four steps give you the opportunity to take a step back from your teaching and look at it through a different lens. As you work your way through the questions and tasks in these steps, remember that you are seeking clarity about the instructional practices that are currently taking place in your classroom. This is a fact-finding mission. Don't beat yourself up or get discouraged if the outcomes you are looking for don't happen overnight. In order to know where to go, you have to know where to start. These first four steps will help you to determine your starting place while also expanding your thinking to move toward a UDL mindset shift.

Tips for Success to Make the UDL Mindset Shift

★ **Take a break:** Feel free to take breaks as needed. Put this book away for a day or two; then pull it back out and keep working.

★ **Answer one question per day:** You don't have to make this shift all at once; one strategy is simply to answer one question per day.

★ **Use another tool:** You don't have to write in the workbook. In fact, you don't have to write at all! If another tool or format will help you process this information, please feel free to use it. I frequently use the voice notes feature on my smartphone. This way I can easily email these voice notes to myself or keep them stored in my phone to access later. Try it out!

★ **Use the following 18-week schedule** to keep you moving through the steps without overwhelming you with too much extra work. If this feels rushed, you can easily change to a 36-week schedule by doubling the weeks for each exercise. Or create another schedule that will work for you!

POSSIBLE 18-WEEK GAME PLAN	
Step 1	
Week 1	Exercise 1: A Certain Kind of Student
Week 2	Exercise 2: Student Success Prerequisites
Week 3	Exercise 3: Big Questions
Week 4	Exercise 4: Come to Terms With It
Step 2	
Week 5	Exercise 1: Your Physical Classroom Space
Week 6	Exercise 2: Your Instructional Preferences
Week 7	Exercise 3: Engagement
Week 8	Exercise 4: Presenting/Teaching Content
Week 9	Exercise 5: Assessments and Activities
Week 10	Exercise 6: Summarize and Synthesize
Step 3	
Week 11	Exercise 1: Pause and Process Your Power
Week 12	Exercise 2: Reflect
Step 4	
Week 13	Exercise 1: Quick Review of Steps 1–3
Week 14	Exercise 2: Check In With Your Emotions
Step 5	
Week 15	Exercise 1: Plus-One Approach
Week 16	Exercise 2: Troubleshooting Approach
Week 17	Exercise 3: Journey-Mapping Approach
Step 6	
Week 18	Exercise 1: Make a Plan
	Exercise 2: Set One Goal for UDL Implementation

Six Steps to Jumpstart Your UDL Practice

Step 1: Recognize It's Not Working for All

Come to terms with the fact that your instruction and classroom environment may be more effective for some learners than for others.

Step 2: Make an Honest Teaching Inventory

Make an honest and thorough inventory of your teaching and learning environment.

Step 3: Acknowledge Your Power

Acknowledge the power you have as a lesson designer and accept the charge to design lessons that enable all students to succeed.

Step 4: Accept That Change Is Possible

Come to believe that a UDL mindset will empower you to design instruction that allows all students to be successful.

Step 5: Seek Out and Reduce Barriers to Engage All Learners

As a result of having a UDL mindset shift, vow to seek out and reduce the learning barriers that get in between your students and their learning.

Step 6: Commit to Design for Equitable Instruction

Commit to using the evidence-based planning framework of UDL to design more equitable instruction that reduces learning barriers and to continue reflecting and refining with student input.

1

Step 1: Recognize It's Not Working for All

Come to terms with the fact that your instruction and classroom environment may be more effective for some learners than for others.

I was recently in a meeting in which my local school board was reviewing our district's standardized testing scores from the last few years (including the year that included remote instruction due to COVID-19). After attendees saw graph after graph that showed some groups of students consistently performing well below other groups, it became abundantly clear that our schools work well for some students, but not for others.

Now, of course, standardized testing is inherently flawed, and in many cases it has been shown to be culturally and linguistically biased. Standardized testing also doesn't take into account things like creativity, kindness, collaborative skills, and so on. Although I am not a big fan of standardized testing, I know that we *can* use these data to help us see, in a quick snapshot, which students are getting what they need in our schools and which are not. Step 1 helps us scale down the big-picture view of instructional efficacy (the effectiveness of our instruction) that we often get from student grades and standardized testing to see what it looks like in our own classrooms.

As you embark on this step, please keep in mind that this is not meant to be a blame game—rather, you're about to begin a fact-finding mission. I'd venture to say that very few educators are teaching all learners equitably. We all have areas in which we can grow, and the next few steps will help us identify where to focus our work. If you start feeling overwhelmed, or feel like you are a terrible teacher, let me clear that up for you right now. You are not a terrible teacher. Teachers who are reflective and who are constantly trying to improve their practice can't possibly be terrible teachers. Maya Angelou, one of America's literary pillars, once said, "Do the best you can until you know better. Then, when you know better, do better." This process will help us to know better so we can do better.

EXERCISE 1:
A Certain Kind of Student

1. Think of one specific student you were *unable* to reach and answer the following questions about that student:

   a. How would you describe the student?

   _____

   _____

   _____

   _____

   _____

   _____

   b. How did this student behave or perform in your class?

   _____

   _____

   _____

   _____

   _____

   _____

c. How did this student's actions or academic performance in your class make you feel?

_____

_____

_____

_____

_____

_____

d. Was this student successful in any other classes (besides yours)?

_____

_____

_____

_____

_____

_____

e. Was this student successful in any arts, athletics, or extracurricular activities?

_____

_____

_____

_____

_____

_____

f. If you answered yes to **d** or **e**, *why* do you think this student was successful in other areas but not in your class? (You do not need to delve into self-criticism, just reflect on this honestly.)

_____

_____

_____

_____

_____

_____

2. Think about students who have been the *most successful* in your class. What underlying circumstances might have *increased* these students' success in your class? Consider their socioeconomic status, gender identity, cultural or racial background, apparent political/religious affiliation, home language, family structure, parental support, ability/disability, and so on.

> **Example:** Most of the students who have been successful in my class are white students, from highly educated, middle- to upper-class, English-speaking families. These are the kinds of students whose parents are able to buy them whatever they need to complete school projects and can even pay for tutoring support. Although all of my students have a specific learning disability, the ones who are most successful in my class have families who are able to support them with medication, therapy, speech therapy, and so on. During COVID lockdown, almost all of my students had a parent who was able to stay at home with them during the day to monitor their schoolwork.

_____

_____

_____

_____

_____

_____

_____

_____

_____

3. Think about students who have been the *least successful* in your class. What underlying circumstances might have *decreased* these students' chances of success in your class? Consider their socioeconomic status, gender identity, cultural or racial background, apparent political/religious affiliation, home language, family structure, parental support, ability/disability, and so on.

> **Example:** The least successful students in my class were those whose families didn't have adequate resources to provide additional support (medication, therapy, etc.). Many of the students who had difficulty in my class are students who talked back or were disrespectful to me. I don't think students' success was based on race or cultural backgrounds, but it's possible that I'm just not attuned to seeking out my own implicit biases and how they play out in my classroom. Honestly, the students who were least successful were the students who didn't respond to my attempts at classroom management. I often attribute this to the students being spoiled, but in all honesty, it may be my own classroom management skills that are at fault.

_____

_____

_____

_____

_____

EXERCISE 2:
Student Success Prerequisites

Check all that apply. To succeed in your class, a student is expected to

Attention and Focus

☐ Pay attention for more than 10 minutes at a time.

☐ Tune out distractions.

☐ Maintain eye contact.

☐ Sit still for more than 10 minutes.

☐ Complete a task they find uninteresting.

☐ Follow multistep directions.

☐ Stay quiet for long periods of time.

☐ Other: _____

Reading and Writing

☐ Read on grade level.

☐ Write on grade level.

☐ Speak English proficiently.

☐ Write in English proficiently.

☐ Other: _____

Study Skills

☐ Know and use good note-taking strategies.

☐ Know and use good test-taking strategies.

☐ Know how to study.

☐ Other: _____

Comprehension

☐ Pull out main ideas.

☐ Make inferences.

☐ Find patterns and relationships.

☐ Remember what they read.

☐ Other: _____

Motivation and Goal Setting

☐ Make connections between content and self.

☐ Set attainable goals.

☐ Differentiate between short-term and long-term goals.

☐ Monitor their own progress.

☐ Persist through challenges.

☐ Other: _____

Memory

☐ Hold information in short-term memory.

☐ Recall information learned previously.

☐ Process information aloud.

☐ Process information on demand.

☐ Other: _____

Communication

- ☐ Ask for help when needed.

- ☐ Speak English.

- ☐ Advocate for their learning needs.

- ☐ Assemble an argument or comment for discussion.

- ☐ Defend a position.

- ☐ Utilize code-switching (e.g., using academic language vs. peer-to-peer language).

- ☐ Respond or answer questions on command.

- ☐ Speak in front of a large group.

- ☐ Other: _____

Hearing/Listening

- ☐ Hear content delivered auditorily.

- ☐ Process content delivered auditorily.

- ☐ Tune out auditory distractions.

- ☐ Regulate own response to auditory stimuli (sounds).

- ☐ Other: _____

Seeing/Watching

- ☐ See content delivered visually.

- ☐ Process content delivered visually.

- ☐ Tune out visual distractions.

- ☐ Regulate own response to visual stimuli.

- ☐ Other: _____

Mobility and Fine-Motor Skills

☐ Walk.

☐ Run.

☐ Stand for long periods of time.

☐ Sit for long periods of time.

☐ Move around the room freely without aid from others.

☐ Use their hands to grasp, pick up, or hold items (writing utensils, beakers, musical instruments, etc.).

☐ Regulate the intensity of their grip.

☐ Write by holding a writing utensil (pencil, pen, etc.).

☐ Keep their hand steady.

☐ Type on a standard keyboard.

☐ Operate a computer mouse or touchpad.

☐ Other: _____

Organization and Time Management

☐ Organize their personal spaces (binders, lockers, backpacks, etc.).

☐ Keep track of multiple items.

☐ Prioritize tasks.

☐ Other: _____

Social-Emotional Skills

☐ Regulate their emotions.

☐ Find a role when working in a group.

☐ Advocate for themselves in a group.

☐ Settle disputes.

☐ Make compromises.

☐ Put the needs of the group above their own.

☐ Read the emotions of others (body language, facial expressions, tone of voice, etc.).

☐ Understand and abide by cultural norms.

☐ Other: _____

Creativity and Problem-Solving

☐ Take appropriate risks.

☐ Ask meaningful questions.

☐ Consider solutions other than their own.

☐ Make novel associations.

☐ Make a hypothesis.

☐ Make prototypes.

☐ Present information clearly and coherently.

☐ Other: _____

EXERCISE 3:
Big Questions

Review your responses to exercises 1 and 2.

1. Are you teaching the students you have or the students you *wish* you had? Explain.

_____

_____

_____

_____

_____

2. Are there students who can't (not won't . . . can't) meet these requirements? If so, what does this mean for these students?

_____

_____

_____

_____

_____

3. Are there students who don't know how to meet these requirements but probably could with a little help? If so, what does this mean for these students?

_____

_____

_____

_____

_____

_____

4. Who is being left behind?

_____

_____

_____

_____

_____

_____

5. Who is flying just under the radar?

_____

_____

_____

_____

_____

_____

EXERCISE 4:
Come to Terms With It

Now that you've answered the questions in exercises 1 and 3, and have gone through the checklist in exercise 2, you have the opportunity to see that the design of your lesson plans or curriculum may not have been as effective for some students as for others. But don't beat yourself up! Remember, some teachers never take the time to consider the effectiveness of their instruction, so you're already winning!

1. Read back through your responses for exercises 1–3. How do you know that your learning environment may not be working as well for some students as it is for others?

_____

_____

_____

_____

_____

_____

_____

_____

_____

_____

_____

Teaching is emotional work.

—DAVID ROSE, cofounder of CAST

2. David Rose's quote speaks the truth! Teaching *is* emotional work! Having come to terms with the fact that your classroom may not be working as well for some students as it is for others, take a few moments to reflect on how this fact makes you feel.

_____

_____

_____

_____

_____

_____

_____

_____

_____

_____

2

Step 2: Make an Honest Teaching Inventory

Make an honest and thorough inventory of your teaching and learning environment.

This step is *huge*! It's huge not only because it's a critical part of developing a UDL mindset, but also because it includes a lot of exercises. This task is similar to the important process of taking inventory at retail stores so that stores have a clear and accurate picture of what is selling, what's not, and what may need to be changed. In an annual or quarterly store inventory, employees count which items they have in stock, which items they are out of, and which items are damaged or no longer necessary. This inventory process can serve as a spring cleaning: a time when stores do a deep-clean of their stock, getting rid of the items that are no longer working, discovering items that may have been misplaced, or returning items that may have been ordered or delivered incorrectly. When businesses are able to put down on paper (or more likely, enter into a spreadsheet) what they actually have, they can then begin to determine what they may need in order to have a fully stocked store.

For this step, we are in search of the truth. And though the sheer number of activities may seem overwhelming, know that you can do them at whatever pace works for you. If you've picked up this book in the middle of the summer or over a longer school break, it may work best for you to knock out all the exercises in a couple days or a week. But if you've arrived at Step 2 in some of the busier months of the school year, be easy on yourself and try to complete one exercise every week or two or at whatever pace is most manageable for you and your schedule.

EXERCISE 1:
Your Physical Classroom Space

1. Grab some colored pencils, markers, or crayons; open your favorite graphic design program; or, if you're into it, draw or make a 3D model of your classroom with whatever you can find.

2. Create and label an aerial view (blueprint) of your classroom.

3. Include all permanent elements, such as:

   ☐ Student seating (desks, tables, etc.)

   ☐ Teacher seating

   ☐ Whiteboard/chalkboard

   ☐ Screen

   ☐ Bookshelves

   ☐ Cabinets

   ☐ Doors

   ☐ Windows

   ☐ Other discipline-specific items (music stands, lab equipment, sinks, etc.)

4. Add items and resources that students might use in the course of a typical day:

   ☐ Pencil sharpener

   ☐ iPads

   ☐ Trash can/recycling

   ☐ Tissues

☐ Extra paper

☐ Extra pencils

☐ Other discipline-specific items (musical instruments, art supplies, calculators, basketballs, etc.)

5. Choose some colors to color-code the following areas:

☐ **Teacher zone:** The area(s) where you spend most of your day (if you're a teacher who likes to circulate, trace your typical circulation path)

☐ **Student zone:** The area(s) where students spend most of their time when in your classroom

☐ **Off-limits to students:** The area(s) in your classroom that are off-limits to students

☐ **Others:**_____

6. Choose a color and circle the following items:

☐ **Areas with high student traffic** (pencil sharpener, trash can, tissues, etc.)

☐ **Areas of distraction** (door to the hallway, windows, etc.)

☐ **Areas where undesirable behavior commonly occurs**

☐ **Areas where students get stuck** (like a bottleneck)

☐ **Others:**_____

7. Take your room map with you and sit in one of the student seats in your classroom. While you are there, draw and label what is in your direct view.

8. Now, pretend you are an *easily distracted student*. Look back at your student-view drawing and ask yourself the following questions:

QUESTIONS	YOUR ANSWERS
What draws my attention?	
What is in between or next to the area where I, the teacher, would stand?	
What is in between or next to the screen or whiteboard?	
Can I see out the door into the hallway?	
Can I see out the windows?	
What other potential distractors do I see?	

9. Now, put yourself in the mind of a student who has sensitivity to sensory stimulation.

Turn on a timer for 1 minute for each of the following check-ins. During this time, close your eyes and do a mental check-in with your senses.

QUESTIONS	YOUR ANSWERS
What do I hear? (Try to parse out and record as many sounds as you can.)	
What do I smell? (Record what you smell.)	
What do I feel? (Consider all sections of your body.) • Temperature • Your joints • Your sitting bones • Other	

10. Look around at the items on your walls.

Think about the students who enter your classroom on a daily basis:

a. Do they see *reflections of themselves* in your classroom?

☐ In the decor

☐ In the selection of materials

☐ In the student work

☐ On the bulletin boards and cork boards

b. Do they see *reflections of your personality* in your classroom?

☐ In the decor

☐ In the materials you have selected

☐ On the bulletin boards and corkboards

c. What else do they see?

_____

_____

_____

_____

_____

_____

_____

_____

EXERCISE 2:
Your Instructional Preferences

Active vs. Passive

1. Look back through your lesson plans and find a day that exemplifies a typical period or day in your classroom.

2. Use graph paper, the following graph, your favorite graphic design or desktop publishing program, or other items of your choosing to visually measure time.

3. To do so, lay out the length of an entire class lesson and make yourself a scale. For example, this is 50 squares long; each square represents 1 minute of a 50-minute class period.

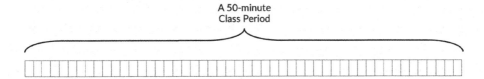

A 50-minute
Class Period

4. Think through your lesson plan and assign each part of the lesson an amount of time. For example, a 50-minute class period in a middle school math class might look something like this:

DURATION	ACTIVITY
5 min.	Bell-ringer activity
10 min.	Check homework
15 min.	Direct instruction: Square roots
10 min.	Demonstrate examples
10 min.	Individual practice

5. Under your laid-out class period, section off the amount of time you have listed for each part of your lesson:

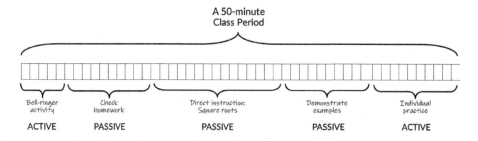

6. Look at each part of your lesson and determine whether each part is active or passive. Write *Active* or *Passive* under each activity.

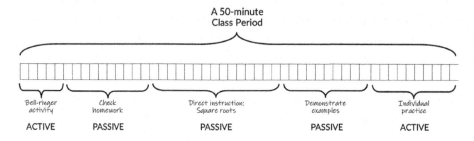

7. Choose a color to represent the following:

☐ Passive student time (time where students are expected to be quiet and sit still)

☐ Active student time (time where students are actively doing something)

8. Color all blocks of time where students are active one color and color all blocks of time where students are passively listening the other color.

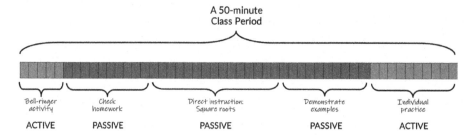

9. Look at your color-blocked class period. What do you notice?

_____

_____

_____

_____

_____

_____

10. How much time are students required to sit still in one spot and listen?

_____

_____

_____

_____

_____

_____

11. Where do the active points in your lesson typically occur?

_____

_____

_____

_____

_____

_____

_____

_____

EXERCISE 3:
Engagement

In this activity, you will ask yourself this very important question: "About what percentage of my students are engaged?" An engaged student is on-task, follows directions, participates with their classmates in actual schoolwork, and is not checking for TikTok and Snapchat updates. They're certainly not asleep. Keep in mind that some students can be on-task but might look like they are not. And remember: This is a fact-finding mission. The goal of this step is to determine the truth about the student experience in your classroom. If you're extra brave, you might even ask students to raise their hands if they're engaged in the task or perhaps ask them to fill out an exit slip letting you know how engaged they felt throughout the class (keep in mind that you may need to define *engagement* for them).

How Engaged Are They?

Task 1: Over the course of one day, take time to purposefully stop teaching every hour on the hour (or use another measurement of time, if that makes more sense) so you can do a quick visual scan of your classroom. About what percentage of your students are engaged?

TIME	% OF STUDENTS WHO ARE ENGAGED

Task 2: Make a copy of your class seating chart. Choose a color to represent the following levels of student engagement, then color, highlight, or shade each student's seat with the appropriate color:

☐ This student is **always** engaged and attentive.

☐ This student is **usually** engaged and attentive.

☐ This student is **sometimes** engaged and attentive.

☐ This student is **rarely** engaged and attentive.

☐ This student is **never** engaged and attentive.

Task 3: Answer the following questions:

1. What choices do students have in your classroom?

_____

_____

_____

_____

_____

_____

2. How do you make topics relevant or interesting to your students?

_____

_____

_____

_____

_____

_____

3. How do you make the learning environment safe (physically and emotionally)?

_____

_____

_____

_____

_____

_____

4. How do you help reduce distractions for your students?

_____

_____

_____

_____

_____

_____

EXERCISE 4:
Presenting/Teaching Content

Task 1: Assign a percentage for each mode of content delivery. In other words, how much of the content you teach is delivered in the following ways? The total should be 100%.

How much of the content in your class is delivered by

_____ Students doing independent reading

_____ You reading to students

_____ Slide presentation

_____ You lecturing to students

_____ Students exploring websites

_____ Print materials other than books (magazines, articles, etc.)

_____ Videos

_____ Examples or demonstrations

_____ Other: _____

_____ Other: _____

_____ Other: _____

_____ Total percentage

Now, translate this percentage breakdown into a pie chart.

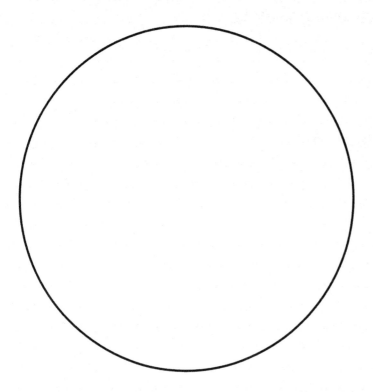

Task 2: Answer the following questions:

1. How do students learn vocabulary in your class?

_____

_____

_____

_____

_____

_____

2. How do you support non-native speakers (i.e., English learners) in your class?

_____

_____

_____

_____

_____

_____

3. How do you teach students (or remind students of) background knowledge?

_____

_____

_____

_____

_____

_____

4. How do you help students identify big ideas, patterns, or themes?

_____

_____

_____

_____

_____

_____

EXERCISE 5: Assessments and Activities

Task 1: Assign a percentage for each mode of assessment you use in your classroom. In other words, how much of the assessment is offered in the following ways? The total should be 100%:

_____ Tests

_____ Quizzes

_____ Papers/essays

_____ Other forms of writing

_____ Presentations/speeches

_____ Projects (build a model, create a replica, paint a still life, etc.)

_____ Demonstrations (labs, coding, etc.)

_____ Performances (plays, skits, concerts, recitals, etc.)

_____ Oral exams

_____ Worksheets

_____ Workbooks

_____ Other: _____

_____ Total percentage

Now, translate this percentage breakdown into a pie chart.

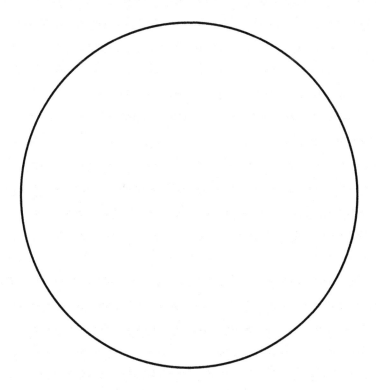

Task 2: Answer the following questions:

1. How do you support all students with scaffolding or supports?

_____

_____

_____

_____

_____

_____

2. How do you determine which students need scaffolding or supports?

_____

_____

_____

_____

_____

_____

3. How do you support students in organizing their materials, managing their time, or setting/monitoring goals?

_____

_____

_____

_____

_____

_____

4. What does formative assessment usually look like in your classroom?

_____

_____

_____

_____

_____

_____

5. What does summative assessment usually look like in your classroom?

_____

_____

_____

_____

_____

_____

_____

_____

_____

_____

EXERCISE 6:
Summarize and Synthesize

Go back and read through all of your responses to exercises 1–5, which asked you to look for ways that your instructional choices might be creating unintentional problems for your students. Look for patterns. What do you notice? Do you see themes or instructional choices popping up multiple times? Pick out a few things (three to five) that really stood out to you, ask yourself the following questions, and record your answers in the following table or in another way (digitally, speech-to-text, etc.) that works for you.

WHAT DID YOU NOTICE? OR WHAT STOOD OUT TO YOU?	WHY DID YOU ORIGINALLY MAKE THIS INSTRUCTIONAL CHOICE?	HOW DOES THIS AFFECT STUDENTS?	IS THIS INSTRUCTIONAL CHOICE SOMETHING YOU CAN CHANGE? (YES OR NO)
Example: I noticed that most of my class time is passive, meaning I expect students to sit and get it.	I think I was worried that if I was not directing all the activities, the students would get out of control.	They get pretty squirmy and they are easily distracted after a couple of classes.	Yes

WHAT DID YOU NOTICE? OR WHAT STOOD OUT TO YOU?	WHY DID YOU ORIGINALLY MAKE THIS INSTRUC-TIONAL CHOICE?	HOW DOES THIS AFFECT STUDENTS?	IS THIS INSTRUC-TIONAL CHOICE SOMETHING YOU CAN CHANGE? (YES OR NO)

3

Step 3: Acknowledge Your Power

Acknowledge the power you have as a lesson designer and accept the charge to design lessons that enable all students to succeed.

Some educators aren't willing to take an honest look at their own instructional practices or to do the hard work of improving them. They go on teaching the same lessons, year after year, never asking themselves if their classroom is a place where students feel empowered or oppressed, brilliant or belittled, capable or culpable. For these teachers, their way is the only way, and if students don't succeed, they'll tell you it's because the students are lazy, defiant, or disrespectful. For these teachers, the problem is the students.

Well, I have bad news for those teachers. If the problem is with the students, then we're all out of luck. There's nothing we can do! You see, we don't *actually* have any control over our students. We're truly powerless over them. Sure, we can dish out rewards and consequences to try to motivate them and keep them in line, but if you think about it, students could get up and walk out of our classrooms at any time, and there's not a lot we could do to stop them. So, the idea that we have control over our students is simply not true. We can't make our students learn. We can't get into their brains and make them read. We can't make them turn in math homework or practice their musical instruments.

But what we *can* do is design our instruction in a way that makes learning easier for students. Not *easier* like dumbing it down . . . *easier* like getting rid of whatever gets in the way of our students' learning. I'm reminded of the famous Serenity Prayer by American theologian Reinhold Niebuhr, which says, ". . . grant me the serenity to accept the things I cannot change, courage to change the things I can, and the wisdom to know the difference."

★ ***What things can't I change? What do I need to accept?*** I may need to accept that I don't actually have control over whether my students learn or not.

★ ***What things do I have the power to change?*** I have the power to help students make connections between what they're learning and their own lives. I have the power to change the way I present content to students. I have the power to change the way I ask students to show what they've learned.

And, as it turns out, when we design our teaching to remove the unnecessary barriers that get in between students and learning, we find that our students are more engaged, more creative, and more intelligent than we ever realized. We have the power to give our students their best chance at success!

EXERCISE 1:
Pause and Process Your Power

Take a few moments to pause and process; then, when you're ready, make yourself two lists:

1. Things you are powerless over in your classroom.

2. Things you have the power to change in your classroom.

Feel free to add more bullet points, continue your list elsewhere, or use another format to organize your two lists.

Things I Am Powerless Over in My Classroom

★ Example: State standards/curriculum

★ Example: If students turn in homework or not

★

★

★

★

★

Things I Have the Power to Change in My Classroom

★ Example: How long students are expected to sit still and listen

★ Example: How I introduce vocabulary

★

★

★

★

★

EXERCISE 2:
Reflect

After you make these two lists, reflect on them. How did these two lists make you feel? What surprised you? What did you uncover? What realizations did you come to?

_____

_____

_____

_____

_____

_____

_____

_____

_____

_____

_____

4

Step 4: Accept That Change Is Possible

Come to believe that a UDL mindset will empower you to design instruction that allows all students to be successful.

As you've worked through the last three steps, you've been guided through the process of thoroughly examining your instructional preferences, your assumptions, and your expectations, and you've looked at your classroom environment through a student lens. Now that you've taken a step back and looked at the information you gathered, it's time to start thinking about solutions.

Step 4 asks us to review our findings from the first three steps and make a conscious decision to shift to a UDL mindset and begin seeking out methods that will allow us to make proactive changes to our classroom and instruction. Keep in mind, the end goal of designing a UDL learning environment is fostering the development of learners who are purposeful, motivated, resourceful, knowledgeable, strategic, and goal-directed through the use of the UDL framework. But in my opinion, the most important reason for rethinking my instructional design is to remove all the obstacles I accidentally placed between my students and learning, so *they* will be able to see, for themselves, how smart, talented, and capable they already are.

EXERCISE 1:
Quick Review of Steps 1–3

1. In Step 1 we looked for evidence to show us that our classrooms might not
    be meeting the needs of all our learners.

    **How do you know that your classroom environment may be more effec-
    tive for some learners than for others?**

    _____

    _____

    _____

    _____

    _____

    _____

    _____

2. When a business takes inventory of their stock, they are trying to find
    out if they have too much of one thing and not enough of another. They
    are also looking for items that are no longer working so they can get
    rid of them and make room for new items that do work. In Step 2, you
    made an honest and thorough inventory of your teaching and learning
    environment.

    What do you have too much of?

    _____

    _____

    _____

_____

_____

_____

_____

_____

What do you *not* have enough of?

_____

_____

_____

_____

_____

What's no longer working that you may need to get rid of?

_____

_____

_____

_____

_____

_____

_____

3. There are a lot of factors that, as teachers, we don't actually have the power to change. However, through our processing and reflection in Step 3, we've found that we actually have the power to build learning environments that give our students the best chance for success. Make a quick summary of your findings from Step 3.

In my classroom I am *powerless* over . . .

_____

_____

_____

_____

_____

In my classroom I *have the power* to . . .

_____

_____

_____

_____

_____

_____

_____

EXERCISE 2:
Check In With Your Emotions

As you contemplate your findings from the first three steps, it is important to acknowledge your emotions about potentially changing your approach to teaching. Take a look at the following chart adapted from the Mood Meter by Marc Brackett, founder of the Yale Center for Emotional Intelligence, and figure out which word best describes your feelings about this process.

Enraged	Panicked	Stressed	Jittery	Shocked	Surprised	Upbeat	Festive	Exhilarated	Ecstatic
Livid	Furious	Frustrated	Tense	Stunned	Hyper	Cheerful	Motivated	Inspired	Elated
Fuming	Frightened	Angry	Nervous	Restless	Energized	Lively	Enthusiastic	Optimistic	Excited
Anxious	Apprehensive	Worried	Irritated	Annoyed	Pleased	Happy	Focused	Proud	Thriller
Repulsed	Troubled	Concerned	Uneasy	Peeved	Pleasant	Joyful	Hopeful	Playful	Blissful
Disgusted	Glum	Disappointed	Down	Apathetic	At Ease	Easygoing	Content	Loving	Fulfilled
Pessimistic	Morose	Discouraged	Sad	Bored	Calm	Secure	Satisfied	Grateful	Touched
Alienated	Miserable	Lonely	Disheartened	Tired	Relaxed	Chilled	Restful	Blessed	Balanced
Despondent	Depressed	Sullen	Exhausted	Fatigued	Mellow	Thoughtful	Peaceful	Comfy	Carefree
Despair	Hopeless	Desolate	Spent	Drained	Sleepy	Complacent	Tranquil	Cozy	Serene

↑ Higher-energy   ↓ Lower-energy

← Unpleasant   Pleasant →

Which word did you select? Why?

_____

_____

_____

_____

_____

_____

In addition to emotional concerns, many teachers have practical concerns about examining their entire approach to teaching (concerns about time, funding, etc.)

What practical concerns are on your mind regarding your UDL mindset shift?

_____

_____

_____

_____

_____

_____

_____

What other questions, comments, or concerns have emerged as you've worked through these first four steps of the UDL mindset shift?

_____

_____

_____

_____

_____

_____

_____

_____

_____

_____

_____

REMINDER:
Check Your Mindset

Do you believe that shifting to (or strengthening) a UDL mindset will empower you to design instruction that allows all students to be successful? Explain.

_____

_____

_____

_____

_____

_____

_____

_____

_____

_____

_____

_____

_____

_____

_____

_____

Congratulations! You've completed a thorough and honest reflection of your instructional practices, you've engaged in the first four steps of your own UDL mindset shift, and you're ready to take on Steps 5 and 6! In part 2 of this book, which covers Steps 5 and 6, you will find three approaches to UDL lesson planning and multiple teaching strategies for implementing UDL into your classroom: the Plus-One approach, the Troubleshooting approach, and the Journey-Mapping approach. These three lesson design approaches give educators systematic ways to consider goals, predict learning barriers, and design to remove those barriers. Finally, part 2 concludes with a section that organizes many teaching strategies with the guidelines and checkpoints that make up the UDL framework.

Part 2

Trying UDL Lesson Design

n the first four steps of this process, you took a close look at the practices and potential barriers in your classroom and instruction. Steps 5 and 6 will give you concrete lesson-planning approaches for proactively removing learning barriers using the UDL framework. The end goal of UDL lesson design is not about retrofitting lessons, it's about intentionally planning instruction to reduce learning barriers from the outset. However, I've found that it can be tricky to make the leap from traditional lesson planning (which is often reactive) to UDL lesson planning (which is always proactive) without providing a bridge that allows teachers to consider how their previous lessons may have unintentionally placed learning barriers in front of students. Once teachers have been awakened to the idea of unintentional learning barriers, they can begin thinking about ways they *could have* or *should have* reduced those barriers. They will then turn these *could haves* and *should haves* into *will dos* as they plan new lessons.

All three lesson design approaches start with an existing lesson and ask teachers to use their experience to evaluate which activities (or parts of the lesson) worked, which didn't, and why. I've found that after using the UDL framework to redesign a few existing lessons, most teachers begin to see and predict the potential learning barriers in their classrooms automatically. The proactive UDL planning process (goals, barriers, design) becomes an ingrained part of their lesson design, and almost without noticing it, teachers find themselves designing totally new UDL lessons that provide students with multiple means of engagement, representation, action, and expression.

5

Step 5: Seek Out and Reduce Barriers to Engage All Learners

As a result of having a UDL mindset shift, you vow to seek out and reduce the learning barriers that get in between your students and their learning.

Now that you've begun to shift your mindset to one that is primed for UDL, you're ready to move on to implementing UDL. This chapter will guide you, step-by-step, through three different approaches to planning lessons with UDL. Each of these approaches will help you move through Step 5 as you uncover these unintentional learning barriers that may be lurking around your instructional environment, causing students to unnecessarily struggle with extraneous aspects that aren't actually involved in the learning itself. Step 5 asks teachers to make a conscious decision to begin the process of identifying barriers to learning that may exist in their current lessons and instructional environment and then make proactive design decisions to remove or reduce those barriers.

When I've presented these three approaches to UDL lesson planning in UDL trainings and workshops with K–12 and higher education instructors, the responses have been overwhelming. I often have participants say things like, "I really love the idea of UDL, but I haven't been able to figure out how to explain it to the other teachers in my building until now. This is exactly what I needed!"

Using the Three Approaches to UDL Lesson Design

Today I can run around 2 miles or so without stopping to walk, but that hasn't always been the case. Sometime around 2013, I decided that I wanted to start running, but I had several barriers: 1) I was *really* out of shape, 2) I couldn't really afford a gym membership, 3) I had small children at home, and 4) I had no idea how to start running. Before 2013, occasionally I had isolated days where I got the idea to "go out for a run," but this usually resulted in me sprinting for about 500 feet, after which I bent over by the side of the road gasping for air. You see, I was trying to go from zero to sixty all at once; I was expecting to be an expert on my first try. After trying this method a couple times and failing, I came to the erroneous conclusion that I simply wasn't a runner. But that was all before 2013.

Sometime in 2013 I saw something on TV that changed my perspective. I can't remember what I was watching, or even on what channel I was watching it. All I remember was that I saw a woman, about my age and overweight, running. Apparently, this woman had lost a ton of weight and was at the point where she could sustain a good 3-mile run without having to stop or walk. When she was interviewed by the host, she explained that she didn't just jump up off the couch one day and run 3 miles; she enlisted the help of a smartphone application that helped her go from sitting on the couch to running a 5K in a period of two to three months. This woman went on to say that the app only required her to run for 60 seconds at a time for the first couple of weeks, after which she walked for 90 seconds; she then alternated between 60-second runs and 90-second walks for a period of 20 minutes, with a 5-minute warm-up walk, and a 5-minute cool-down walk.

For some reason, this gradual, step-by-step way of building up endurance and stamina for running had never occurred to me. This chance encounter with some random television interview completely changed my mindset about running. I decided to give it a try, and today I am able to run for 30–45 minutes at a time—something that would have been unthinkable to me before I heard this woman share her experience, strength, and hope. For me, the key was starting small with one manageable running/walking plan, and then building on that plan over a period of several months until I was comfortable running for longer periods of time.

When my running mindset shifted, I had the desire and motivation to run. But I still needed a starter program to get myself into the habit of running, so I enlisted help from a smartphone app that scaffolded this process for me. Doing the app program wasn't my end goal. Being able to run, without walking, for a 30- to 45-minute period of time wasn't even the end goal! What I really wanted was to *get in shape*.

After several months of running without changing anything else (diet, sleep, caffeine intake, etc.), I hadn't lost much weight, and I definitely wasn't in shape! I realized that in order to be "in shape," I would have to look at other parts of my lifestyle for problems in my health practices. It took several years of troubleshooting and slowly removing more and more barriers to finally get to a place where I felt like I was in shape. I finally got to the point where running, eating healthily, getting plenty of rest, and drinking lots of water had become second nature.

Why am I sharing my story about getting in shape? Because the analogy connects nicely with the route some educators may need to take in order to start on their UDL journey.

For many teachers, using an incremental approach to designing lessons, like the Plus-One approach (Tobin & Behling, 2018), can transform the way they think about teaching. The Plus-One approach may be your "Couch to 5K"–type app to help you begin thinking like a universal learning designer, but don't stop there! You're just beginning!

After you've shifted your thinking and begun to see some positive benefits of using an incremental design strategy like the Plus-One approach, you can move on in your UDL journey by taking a closer look at your teaching practices using the Troubleshooting approach. This approach starts when you acknowledge a problem you're seeing in your classroom; it helps you reframe that problem and use the UDL framework to find solutions that will help you reduce learning barriers so that all students can thrive. The third and final approach, Journey Mapping (Ducharme, 2016), will guide you through the process of examining your teaching through the eyes of the end users, your students. This peek into the design-thinking world utilizes the user experience (UX) to inform instructional decisions, and it helps teachers keep their focus on learners and learner variability.

The following sections will take you through these three design approaches: the Plus-One approach, the Troubleshooting approach, and the Journey-Mapping approach. If you follow these approaches, you will be even closer to your end goal of reducing learning barriers for your students!

Which Approach Is Right for Me?

While working with educators on UDL implementation, I have come across three distinct types of teachers: 1) teachers who are excited and ready to learn about UDL, 2) teachers who are *not* interested in UDL, and 3) teachers who like the ideas of UDL but have difficulty seeing how they can possibly make it work in their classroom.

For teachers like the last one (whom I like to call the *reluctant teacher*), the idea of implementing UDL in their classroom may be overwhelming. If you've always been a very structured teacher, the idea of using something like flexible seating or choice assignments may be the classroom equivalent of my 3-mile run! It's so far from what normally happens in your classroom that it's difficult to even fathom how to go from where you are to where you may think UDL-utopia is.

The good news is this: You can start by making one small change at a time! You don't have to go from sitting on the couch to being able to run a 5K overnight! In fact, UDL seems to work well when teachers try one thing, evaluate how it went, and then redesign as needed based on the results.

Can I handle an entire redesign of my classroom and a total overhaul of my entire teaching career all at once? Um . . . *no!* But can I handle keeping everything the same and changing one thing at a time? Yes! That's totally doable.

As with building good habits in general, these habits of practice and habits of mind can point us in the right direction—the UDL direction. Does adding one or two habits mean I'm "doing" UDL? No, definitely not. But it does mean I'm beginning to think with the intentional, learner-centered, goal-focused mindset that UDL requires. Over the next several pages, you will learn how the Plus-One approach can be used to ease your way into designing instruction that will benefit the variety of learners you have in your classroom.

Plus-One Approach: Building Student Choices

In 2018, as I was reading Thomas J. Tobin and Kirsten T. Behling's 2018 book, *Reach Everyone, Teach Everyone: Universal Design for Learning in Higher Education,* I encountered an approach to UDL that mirrored my running experience. The authors called it plus-one thinking:

> Instead of focusing on the three brain networks, think of UDL as merely plus-one thinking about the interactions in your course. Is there just one more way

that you can help keep learners on task, just one more way that you could give them information, just one more way that they could demonstrate their skills? (p. 134).

It can be very easy to get overwhelmed by the neuroscience and research foundations of the UDL framework. (Full disclosure: Before the 2018 redesign of the CAST UDL Guidelines website, I had to, on several occasions, look up definitions and synonyms for some of the words in the UDL Guidelines. I mean, what the heck does *heighten salience* even mean?! I get it now, but it took me a while—like several books, conferences, and years of studying UDL—to get to a place where I felt like I fully understood the UDL Guidelines.) The reason I love the Plus-One approach is that it makes UDL manageable.

You will find elementary and middle school examples of instruction designed with the Plus-One approach, along with blank templates, at the end of this section and a printable blank template on the *tinyurl.com/ TransformWithUDL* website.

How Plus-One Works

CONSIDER YOUR GOAL.

The Gist:

Before making changes to your classroom or instruction, consider what your goal or motivation is for wanting to make these changes.

What to Do:

1. Think about any problems or concerns you have encountered in your class that could be helped by UDL. Ask yourself, "What's not quite working the way I want it to?"

2. Look at your Plus-One Approach template. This template has space to think through three different problems—one per row.

3. In the top-left space (Goal), add the goal you have for your classroom or teaching.

Tips and Tricks:

★ Remember: Your goal can be about any problem you've encountered in the process of teaching and learning.

For Example:

Let's consider the problem one middle school language arts teacher encountered: Some of their students were having difficulty keeping up with the novel they were reading as a class. So, for this teacher, the goal might be for all students to be able to read the novel.

GOAL	LAST YEAR/ SEMESTER	THIS YEAR/ SEMESTER	NEXT YEAR/ SEMESTER
All students will be able to read an entire novel.	1.	1. 2.	1. 2. 3.

CONSIDER WHAT YOU DID LAST YEAR.

The Gist:

It's important to think about what you have already done for this particular learning activity or scenario in the past.

What to Do:

1. Think about your goal. What are you already doing or what have you always done in relation to this goal? Think of your goal as a starting point.

2. Look at your Plus-One Approach template. In the same row as your goal, find the box under the column labeled Last Year/Semester and add what you're already doing in relation to this goal.

3. Now copy the same text you've written under number 1 in the Last Year/Semester column into the number 1 spot for each of the other two columns.

Tips and Tricks:

★ This suggestion to review your goals is not meant to cause feelings of guilt or shame; this is merely a starting point. When you've determined where you are starting, you can make more-informed decisions about what to add next.

For Example:

Let's think more about our language arts example. This teacher has always given students a paper copy of the novel the class is reading (which stays in the teacher's classroom). The students read the book individually during quiet reading time. So, in the Plus-One Approach template, under Last Year/Semester, this teacher might add "Students read the book to themselves."

GOAL	LAST YEAR/ SEMESTER	THIS YEAR/ SEMESTER	NEXT YEAR/ SEMESTER
All students will be able to read an entire novel.	1. Students read the book to themselves.	1. Students read the book to themselves. 2.	1. Students read the book to themselves. 2. 3.

THINK ABOUT THIS YEAR.

The Gist:

Now, you're ready to take another small step by adding one thing to what you are already doing in relation to your goal.

What to Do:

1. Look at the goal you have written in your Plus-One Approach template and reread it to yourself.

2. Ask yourself, "Is there any other possible way to accomplish this goal?"

3. Ask your students, "What would help you be able to accomplish this goal?"

4. In your Plus-One Approach template, add your second idea in the number two slot under This Year/Semester, and again in the number two slot for Next Year/Semester.

For Example:

In the language arts example, the teacher is able to find an audiobook version of the novel, so in the number two slot, she adds "Students listen to the audiobook version." Upon reflection, it occurs to the teacher that having an audiobook version of a class novel would have been really helpful a few years ago when she had a student in her class who was blind. This particular student had to have a paraeducator sit next to him and whisper the book to him during silent reading time. The teacher realized that if she had provided the audiobook version to the student who was blind, he wouldn't have had to rely on a paraeducator. He could have been in control of his own learning. The language arts teacher keeps this scenario in mind and begins to consider finding or recording audio versions for other reading excerpts she plans to use later in the school year.

GOAL	LAST YEAR/ SEMESTER	THIS YEAR/ SEMESTER	NEXT YEAR/ SEMESTER
All students will be able to read an entire novel.	1. Students read the book to themselves.	1. Students read the book to themselves. 2. Students listen to the audiobook version.	1. Students read the book to themselves. 2. Students listen to the audiobook version. 3.

PLAN FOR NEXT YEAR.

The Gist:

Here's one more option for giving students three choices instead of none.

What to Do:

1. Take a look back at the goal and the first two options you have listed on the first row of your Plus-One Approach template and ask yourself, "Who am I leaving out?" In other words, "Have I considered the needs, talents, interests, culture, racial background, circumstances, and variability of all the students I teach?"

2. Ask your students, "What else would help you be able to accomplish this goal?"

3. Determine one more way you can provide options for this goal and add it in the third column, labeled Next Year/Semester, in the slot for number three.

Tips and Tricks:

★ One way to help you think of ideas is to look over your class rosters or seating charts while comparing the options you have listed. Are there any students for whom these options wouldn't work? Seeing the names, and picturing their faces, is a great way to jog your memory.

For Example:

The language arts teacher has noticed that some students are still having difficulty staying focused while reading or while listening to the audiobook version of the novel. Many of these students are still learning English. She wonders if a version of the novel that utilizes some visual elements might be helpful in conveying the characters and plot of the novel. Luckily, the teacher is able to locate and order a few copies of a graphic novel version of the book. In slot 3 of her Plus-One Approach template she adds "Students read the graphic novel."

GOAL	LAST YEAR/ SEMESTER	THIS YEAR/ SEMESTER	NEXT YEAR/ SEMESTER
All students will be able to read an entire novel.	1. Students read the book to themselves.	1. Students read the book to themselves. 2. Students listen to the audiobook version.	1. Students read the book to themselves. 2. Students listen to the audiobook version. 3. Students read the graphic novel.

REFLECT AND ADJUST.

The Gist:

Now you may want to try out your This Year/Semester addition and reflect on how it went.

What to Do:

1. After you have filled out your Plus-One Approach template, implement the addition you chose for your This Year/Semester plan in your classroom for a few months or up to an entire year or semester—make sure you try it for enough time to work out the kinks and get a good feel for its effectiveness.

2. Reflect:

   ★ From your own perspective, how did it go?

   ★ What were the students' impressions of this addition?

   ★ Did the addition of a new option help you meet your goal?

   ★ If it went well, are there ways you could improve or streamline?

   ★ If it didn't go well, why do you think it went awry? Was it the new addition that didn't work, or were students not prepped enough for the change?

3. If the addition you made worked well, keep it! If it didn't, either adjust it or toss it out.

4. Once you feel comfortable implementing your options from last year/semester and this year/semester, add the option you chose for next year/semester, and repeat the directions in this step.

For Example:

The teacher in our example reflects on her additions and decides to keep all three versions. She found that one of her students who has a dyslexia diagnosis participated much more frequently in class after being provided with the option of using the audiobook version of the novel. She also noticed that some of her students with attentional barriers (ADHD, executive function issues, etc.) were much more engaged with the graphic novel version, and one student even went back and reread a chapter in the original paperback novel so they could compare the two versions. After encountering multiple snow days this semester, the language arts teacher decides to upload a PDF version of this book to the classroom's website for the coming grading period so students can access the written version of the book from any internet-capable device.

Final Thoughts on the Plus-One Approach

It is important to keep in mind that the Plus-One approach should not be the end of your UDL design journey. Adding choice for the sake of choice isn't the same as proactively designing instruction to reduce learning barriers. Remember, when I wanted to get in shape, I didn't just use the smartphone app and stop there; I kept moving forward, uncovering more and more barriers until I felt I had achieved my goal. The same is true of UDL. The goal of UDL isn't simply to give students choices. It is to design instruction that removes barriers so students can move closer to becoming expert learners.

The following tables include a few more elementary school and middle school examples of ways to use the Plus-One approach along with a blank version of the Plus-One Approach template.

+1 Plus-One Approach

ES: Elementary School Examples

Goal	Last Year/ Semester	This Year/ Semester	Next Year/ Semester
Reading: Provide students with multiple ways to read texts.	1. Read individually.	1. Read individually. 2. Read graphic novel version.	1. Read individually. 2. Read graphic novel version. 3. Listen to audio book version.
Classroom Library: Expand classroom library by adding more "Who Was" books about famous people of color.	1. - MLK - Harriet Tubman	1. - MLK - Harriet Tubman 2. - Pele - Tuskegee Airmen	1. - MLK - Harriet Tubman 2. - Pele - Tuskegee Airmen 3. - Selena - Venus & Serena Williams
Arts-infused Lessons: Teach more arts-infused lessons.	1. "Turn a historic scene into a comic strip" lesson.	1. "Turn a historic scene into a comic strip" lesson. 2. 1 Creative writing lesson based on a painting	1. "Turn a historic scene into a comic strip" lesson. 2. 1 Creative writing lesson based on a painting 3. Partner with music teacher to plan a co-taught unit.

+1 Plus-One Approach

Goal	Last Year/	This Year/	Next Year/
Group Work: Provide students with opportunities to work in groups.	1. Students work individually.	1. Students do most work individually. 2. Plan one group project.	1. Students do some work individually. 2. Plan one group project. 3. Grading period study partners
Communication: Build stronger communication with families.	1. Email parents to introduce myself at start of year.	1. Email parents to introduce myself at start of year. 2. Check-in phone call with parents after 1st month.	1. Email parents to introduce myself at start of year. 2. Check-in phone call with parents after 1st month. 3. Receive texts from families via a reminder app.
Study Skills: Explicitly teach study skills.	1. Students get a grade for turning in notes.	1. Students get a grade for turning in notes. 2. Make flashcards & play flashcard games in class.	1. Students get a grade for turning in notes. 2. Make flashcards & play flashcard games in class. 3. Teach students to use their own mnemonics for memorization.

+1 Plus-One Approach

Goal	Last Year/ Semester	This Year/ Semester	Next Year/ Semester
	1.	1. 2.	1. 2. 3.
	1.	1. 2.	1. 2. 3.
	1.	1. 2.	1. 2. 3.

Copyright 2020, J. Pusateri

Troubleshooting Approach: Solving Problems of Practice

Troubleshooting guides are used in all kinds of fields and settings; they can be extremely helpful in solving problems, especially when you see a problem but aren't quite sure of its cause. For example, a troubleshooting guide in the back of a car manual helps a user figure out why a warning light has appeared on the dashboard. Troubleshooting guides are also commonly posted online to help solve technology problems. But one of the most delicious forms of a troubleshooting guide is a simple, but surprisingly helpful, guide that helps would-be bakers diagnose problems with their chocolate chip cookies.

All of these different troubleshooting guides have one thing in common. They start with the problem (e.g., Why are my cookies so flat?), and the problem then points us to the solution (avoid using all granulated sugar).

But why are troubleshooting guides so helpful? Well, in most cases, it's because the troubleshooting guide meets the user where they are.

When I'm dealing with a warning light that suddenly appears on the dashboard of my car, I go straight to the troubleshooting section of the manual—the rest of the car manual is of no help to me because I don't even know where to start! I guess I could look at the section about the braking system, but I don't actually know whether the problem actually lies in the braking system. Or, I could look at the oil pressure, but does the oil pressure even cause a warning light to come on? In most scenarios, I have no idea what the cause is, so it doesn't help me to look at the individual sections. However, the one thing I *do* know is that there is a problem. And that is exactly where the troubleshooting guide meets me. At the problem. The popular website WebMD does the same thing. It asks users for the known aspects of their ailment: their symptoms. The WebMD program then asks a series of questions to help people narrow down their possible ailment based on their symptoms to just a few possible causes. The UDL framework can serve the same purpose: Educators can use problems of practice in the classroom to point them toward evidence-based solutions. The pages that follow lead teachers through a step-by-step process for using the UDL framework as a troubleshooting guide that will help diagnose and find solutions for problems of practice in the classroom.

You will find elementary and middle school examples of instruction designed with the Troubleshooting approach, along with a blank template, at the end of this section and a printable blank template on the *tinyurl.com/ TransformWithUDL* website. What follows is a completed version of a first-grade lesson that will be referred to throughout this section.

Troubleshooting Approach

Elementary School Example (1st Grade)

① The Problem: Name It & Reframe It

Name the problem:

The students keep blurting out answers without raising their hands.

Reframe the problem:

Remember: This part shouldn't refer to the student(s).

The design of the classroom structure does not provide enough practice for norms, protocols, and procedures.

② Match the Problem with a UDL Guideline

Which one of the 9 UDL Guidelines does this most closely align with?

- ☐ Recruiting Interest
- ☐ Sustaining Effort & Persistence
- ☑ Self Regulation
- ☐ Perception
- ☐ Language & Symbols
- ☐ Comprehension
- ☐ Physical Action
- ☐ Expression & Communication
- ☐ Executive Functions

③ Narrow Guideline to UDL Checkpoint

Which checkpoint is most relevant to the problems I'm seeing in this class?

Write the checkpoint text here:

Facilitate personal coping skills & strategies
(9.2– Self Regulation)

Ask the students: Is this the problem? Summarize students' responses here:

-They said they get so excited when they know the right answer that they can't wait to tell me. Aw.

④ Find UDL-Aligned Strategies

Strategies you already know that align with your checkpoint:

1. Tell them to "clip down" every time they don't wait to be called on.

2. Try to limit the number of questions I ask to avoid the problem.

New strategies to try:

1. Quiet Sign Hand Raise-
Have them "raise their hand" by holding their index finger in front of their lips when they know the answer

2. Countdown to Answering-
Count aloud from 10-0 after they ask a question, then they take answers.

⑤ Reflect & Adjust

How did the strategy go?

We tried the "Quiet Sign Hand Raise", and it worked really well! The act of placing their finger in front of their lips reminded them to wait quietly to be called on.

Note: Raising hands only lets 1 student answer at a time. I'd like to find ways for more students to be able to answer.

Ask the students:

They thought it was fun to raise their hand in a different way, and one student wanted to make a different "raise hand" motion every day.

How Troubleshooting Works

IDENTIFY PROBLEMS OF PRACTICE.

The Gist:

This step helps teachers discover the actual problem in the design and reframe it in a way that aligns with UDL.

NOTE **This approach will be more easily understood if you can make a copy of the blank Troubleshooting Approach template at the end of this section and fill it out along with the following instructions.**

What to Do:

When we are new to UDL, we may have difficulty connecting the problems we see occurring with our students to the learning barriers that are built into the design of the environment and instruction. One way to help make this connection is by asking ourselves, "What does the problem look like?" Because we see the symptoms of the problem play out in students' engagement, behavior, and performance, it can *look* like the problem is with the student. So, to simulate this, we will write the problem as if the barrier is in the student. Yes, it feels a little yucky because one of the first things we learn about UDL is that the problem *isn't* in the student, but you're just going to have to trust me for a minute.

1. Write what the problem looks like in the Step 1 box of the template under the heading Name the Problem. Answers to this question often have students as the subject of the sentence, with words like *They*, *The students*, *She*, and *He*:

   ★ "They won't stop talking!"

   ★ "She isn't turning homework in."

   ★ "These students don't know how to study."

   ★ "They aren't doing the readings."

   ★ "He's just goofing off the whole time."

2. Underline the subject of the sentence.

3. Once you've named the problem, you're ready to reframe it into more UDL-friendly terms by filling out the Reframe the Problem part of Step 1.

4. In the first part of Step 1, the subject of our problem sentence was the students, which implied that the barrier was in the students. Luckily, we know that this isn't the case. UDL tells us that the barrier is in the design of the learning environment and instruction. In order to reframe the problem we listed in the first part of Step 1, we start our new sentence with a subject that indicates that the barrier is in the design. Here are some good ways to start this sentence:

   ★ "The design of the lesson doesn't provide for…"

   ★ "The learning activities aren't…"

   ★ "The location of the materials isn't…"

   ★ "The lesson hasn't built in scaffolding for…"

5. Once you've reframed the problem to show that the barrier is in the environment or instruction rather than in the student, write it in the bottom of Step 1 under the section labeled Reframe It.

6. Finally, underline the new subject of this sentence.

Tips and Tricks:

★ Yes, I know that writing out a problem and blaming it on the student feels bad (especially if you've been working with UDL for a while), but for the purposes of discovering the real problem, go ahead and write what the problem looks like. If it helps, think about how another, non-UDL teacher might try to describe the problem. Or, you can consider how one teacher might describe the problem to another during a lunch chat in the teacher workroom.

★ Reframing the problem of practice can be a little tricky, so don't get discouraged if you don't catch on right away. Here are a couple more examples:

BEFORE (THE PROBLEM IS WITH THE STUDENT.)	AFTER (THE PROBLEM IS WITH THE DESIGN.)
"If <u>Brayden</u> could read better, he'd do much better in social studies class."	"<u>The design</u> of the social studies class only provides students with one option (reading a textbook) for learning content."
"<u>These students</u> just don't care about algebra."	"<u>The learning activities</u> don't highlight the connections between the content and students' interests and values."

For Example:

Let's consider a first-grade classroom. This class's teacher names the problem by stating that "The students keep blurting out answers without raising their hands." He goes back and underlines the subject of that sentence, "The students." As our teacher reframes the problem, he realizes that perhaps students aren't raising their hands and waiting until they are called on because they haven't yet learned this skill. He had assumed this was a skill they had learned in kindergarten and remembered over the summer. He decides to reframe the problem as "The design of the classroom structure does not provide enough practice for norms, protocols, and procedures." Finally, he underlines the subject—in this case, "The design"—and checks to make sure the new subject doesn't include the students.

MATCH THE PROBLEM WITH UDL GUIDELINES.

The Gist:

Decide which UDL Guideline aligns most closely to the problem.

What to Do:

1. Look through the nine UDL Guidelines and ask yourself, "What is this problem really about?"

ENGAGEMENT	REPRESENTATION	ACTION & EXPRESSION
Recruiting Interest	Perception	Physical Action
Sustaining Effort & Persistence	Language & Symbols	Expression & Communication
Self Regulation	Comprehension	Executive Functions

2. In the Troubleshooting Approach template, check the box next to the UDL Guideline that you think most closely aligns to your problem of practice.

Tips and Tricks:

★ If you're having trouble, you can begin by crossing out the guidelines that don't apply to your problem.

★ It is possible to find yourself stuck between two different guidelines. If this happens, don't panic! Remember, this is an iterative process, so choose whichever guideline feels right in your gut. If you troubleshoot a problem using one guideline, and the strategies don't seem to help, simply start the process again using the other guideline.

For Example:

Our teacher has identified that "The design of the classroom structure does not provide enough practice for norms, protocols, and procedures." After looking at all nine UDL Guidelines he determines that this problem most closely aligns with the Self Regulation UDL Guideline, so he places a checkmark in Step 2 of the Troubleshooting Approach template next to Self Regulation.

NARROW THE GUIDELINE TO A UDL CHECKPOINT.

If the guideline (the word in bold in the following image—in this case, Self Regulation) helps us determine the problem, then we can think of the checkpoints (the bulleted phrases below the guideline) as the possible solutions.

The Gist:

Take a closer look at the UDL Guideline associated with your problem and try to find one checkpoint that you think would be most helpful.

What to Do:

Now that you've figured out which UDL Guideline you think most closely aligns with your problem, it's time to narrow the solution down further by looking at the checkpoints (bulleted lists) under your UDL Guideline. You can do this by looking at the copy of the UDL framework in the appendix or by visiting the CAST UDL Guidelines website *http://udlguidelines.cast.org/*.

1. Look through each of the bulleted checkpoints in the UDL Guideline associated with your problem and think about your class. Ask yourself, "Which of these things is most relevant to the problems I'm seeing in this class?"

2. Add the text of the checkpoint you've chosen in your Troubleshooting Approach template.

3. Then, ask the students if the checkpoint you've selected is what's causing the problem, and record their answer. Students probably won't understand what you're asking if you just read, word for word, the text from the UDL framework, so you may need to adjust the language according to the students you teach.

Tips and Tricks:

★ Don't be intimidated by the language; it's not as scary as it may first appear. You can get a little more information on what each checkpoint means by clicking the checkpoint on the CAST UDL Guidelines interactive website: *http://udlguidelines.cast.org/*.

For Example:

As our first-grade teacher thinks about the problems he's seen with students blurting out answers, he determines that he hasn't given students very many opportunities to practice what to do when they have something they want to say out loud. He determines that this problem is really about students needing help with facilitating coping skills and strategies around self-regulation, so he adds this checkpoint (9.2) in the top part of Step 3 in his Troubleshooting Approach template. Then, he says this to the students: "Friends, I have a question for you. Do you remember how we sometimes forget to raise our hands before we talk out loud? I wonder why we keep forgetting to raise our hands and wait to be called on. Why do you think we do this?" Students share that sometimes they get so excited when they know the answer that they can't wait to tell the teacher so they say it really fast and forget to raise their hands. He asks them if they think it would help if they practiced some different ways to help them remember to raise their hands, and they agree that it would. The teacher writes down students' responses in the bottom of Step 3.

FIND UDL-ALIGNED STRATEGIES.

The Gist:

Once they have diagnosed the problem, teachers can begin to pull from their own toolbox of instructional strategies or use online resources to locate strategies that may help remove learning barriers for students.

What to Do:

1. Use the CAST UDL Guidelines interactive website (*http://udlguidelines.cast.org/*) to read a little more information about your selected checkpoint.

Super Important Stuff

Remember, there's no such thing as a *UDL strategy*. The UDL framework helps us to know which teaching actions are most effective for the learning brain. But teachers can use *many* strategies to take those teaching actions. For example, checkpoint 7.1 tells us that to recruit interest, we should optimize individual choice and autonomy. Well, how many different ways can you think of (off the top of your head) to provide students with choice? You can probably think of lots of ways, right? The strategies you find in the websites listed here, and those in part 3 of this book, represent just *some* of the ones that you can use to take the teaching actions suggested in the UDL Guidelines.

2. Consider the various strategies you have learned as a teacher. What instructional tools are in your toolbox from your teacher certification program? From professional development (PD) trainings? From conferences you attended? From articles or books you have read? From your own trial and error? Which of these strategies might help you to address the problems you diagnosed earlier? Add one or two strategies you already know in the top portion of Step 4.

3. Take a few moments to review K–8 online resources, and strategies listed in part 3 of this book, which tie evidence-based strategies to UDL Guidelines and checkpoints:

   a. CAST UDL Guidelines Interactive Website: *http://udlguidelines.cast.org/*

b. UDL Goalbook App: *https://goalbookapp.com/toolkit/v/strategies*

c. UDL for Teachers: *https://udlforteachers.com/*

Please note: You can do an internet search for the UDL Guidelines, but sometimes you will accidentally pull up older versions. These three sources will take you to the 2018 version of the CAST UDL Guidelines, which, at the writing of this book, is the most current version.

4. Add one or two new strategies from one of these UDL resources to the bottom portion of the Step 4 strategies box.

Tips and Tricks:

★ For now, don't worry about trying to find the perfect strategy. It doesn't exist. Rather, focus on finding a strategy that your students will actually use and that you genuinely like.

★ Remember, building in UDL-aligned strategies may take a bit more time in the planning phase, but these strategies usually pay off when we don't have to refocus students and reteach content.

For Example:

Let's return to our first-grade teacher whose students are having difficulty with self-regulation related to facilitating personal coping skills and strategies (checkpoint 9.2). First, the teacher adds two strategies he's used before that might help remove learning barriers pertaining to this checkpoint in the top part of Step 4 in the Troubleshooting Approach template:

★ **Clip Chart:** Tell students to "clip down" every time they don't wait to be called on.

★ **Limiting Questions:** Try to limit the number of questions I ask to avoid the problem.

After looking through several strategies on the CAST UDL Guidelines interactive website, the Goalbook App website, and the UDL for Teachers website, our example teacher found two that he thinks will work especially well with this age group and the personalities within his class:

★ **Quiet Sign Hand Raise:** Have them "raise their hand" by holding their index finger in front of their lips when they know the answer.

★ **Countdown to Answering:** Count aloud backward from 10 to 0 after I ask a question, then take answers.

REFLECT AND ADJUST.

The Gist:

Try one or more of the strategies in your classroom and reflect on how those strategies worked for you and your students. Then, ask the students for their feedback on how the strategy is working from their perspective.

What to Do:

1. Try one or more of your strategies with your class.
2. Take a few moments to reflect on how this strategy worked in your classroom. Record your thoughts in the top of Step 5 on your Troubleshooting Approach template.
3. Ask the students how this strategy is working for them and record their feedback in the bottom of Step 5 on your Troubleshooting Approach template.

Tips and Tricks:

★ It can be helpful to let students know that you are trying something new and that you are okay if the activity doesn't work out. But mostly, you want their input on how the new lesson worked or didn't work for their learning. Students often enjoy being part of your instructional design process, and including them is also an opportunity for you to model how to take healthy risks.

★ Your personal reflection doesn't need to be lengthy. Simply writing down a few words to describe how the lesson went will help you to process your emotions and analyze the instruction.

For Example:

The first-grade teacher tried the Quiet Sign Hand Raise strategy and it worked really well. He mentions that the physical motion of putting their fingers in front of their mouths reminds the students to wait to speak. He also realizes that having students raise their hands to answer limits the number of students that get to answer questions out loud, and he mentions that he'd like to try to find some whole-class participation methods so more students get to answer each question. The teacher records these reflections in the top part of the Troubleshooting Approach template. Then, he asks the students how the Quiet Sign Hand Raise is working and they say they liked it. In fact, one student asks if they can try to make up new hand motions for raising their hand every day! The teacher records this feedback in the Troubleshooting Approach template.

Final Thoughts for the Troubleshooting Approach

Remember, problems of practice will constantly emerge (regardless of how long we've been teaching) because we are always encountering new students, new content, new barriers, and new challenges in our classroom. The Troubleshooting approach can help you break down these problems of practice through a systematic approach to problem-solving in your own classroom. UDL is an iterative process, so keep on designing and optimizing your instruction!

The following tables include two more examples of lessons that have been redesigned with the Troubleshooting approach and a blank version of the Troubleshooting Approach template.

Troubleshooting Approach

Elementary School Example (5th Grade)

1 The Problem:
Name It & Reframe It

Name the problem:

They don't understand how the U.S. Government's checks & balances works. I've explained it many times, but they just don't get it.

Reframe the problem:

Remember: This part shouldn't refer to the student(s).

The delivery of the content is not aligning with the students' learning needs.

2 Match the Problem with a UDL Guideline

Which one of the 9 UDL Guidelines does this most closely align with?

☐ Recruiting Interest

☐ Sustaining Effort & Persistence

☐ Self Regulation

☐ Perception

☐ Language & Symbols

☑ Comprehension

☐ Physical Action

☐ Expression & Communication

☐ Executive Functions

3 Narrow Guideline to UDL Checkpoint

Which checkpoint is most relevant to the problems I'm seeing in this class?

Write the checkpoint text here:

Activate or supply background knowledge.
(3.1- Comprehension)

Ask the students: Is this the problem? Summarize students' responses here:

-They said they get confused about which branch does which job.

- Also, they can't remember the difference between the House and the Senate.

4 Find UDL-Aligned Strategies

Strategies you already know that align with your checkpoint:

1. Watch a video to review background knowledge.

2. Use a pre-test to see what info they do and don't know.

New strategies to try:

1. Concept Map
   Have students create a concept map that visually shows the checks & balances between the 3 branches of US government.

2. K-W-L Chart
   Students brainstorm what they KNOW, what they WANT to know and what they LEARNED.

5 Reflect & Adjust

How did the strategy go?

We watched a video, but it still didn't seem like they understood. So, we made concept maps where students had to include the 3 branches, and color-coded, labeled arrows between them. This seemed to really help clarify checks & balances for them.

Ask the students:

My students always like anything that includes drawing, so they enjoyed the concept maps, and they said seeing the stuff visually really helped them remember the differences.

Troubleshooting Approach

Middle School Example (6th Grade)

1 The Problem: Name It & Reframe It

Name the problem:

They keep forgetting to bring their materials to class (binder, notebook, pencil, etc.).

Reframe the problem:
Remember: This part shouldn't refer to the student(s)

The design does not have built-in supports to help with pre-planning, organization, and time management.

2 Match the Problem with a UDL Guideline

Which one of the 9 UDL Guidelines does this most closely align with?

- [ ] Recruiting Interest
- [ ] Sustaining Effort & Persistence
- [ ] Self Regulation
- [ ] Perception
- [ ] Language & Symbols
- [ ] Comprehension
- [ ] Physical Action
- [ ] Expression & Communication
- [x] Executive Functions

3 Narrow Guideline to UDL Checkpoint

Which of the checkpoints (bulleted items) is most relevant to the problems I'm seeing in this class?

Write the checkpoint text here:

Facilitate managing information and resources. (6.3– Executive Functions)

Ask the students: Is this the problem? Summarize the students' responses here:

-They said that they forget which stuff they are supposed to bring on which days.

-They also said they forget which materials they need for which cases.

4 Find UDL-Aligned Strategies

Strategies you already know that align with your checkpoint:

1. Taking points away for not having materials

2. Giving bonus points for bringing materials

New strategies to try:

1. B.Y.O. List-
   Post a BYO (bring your own) list outside my door with materials needed for each class period that day. Post before the day starts.
2. Stop Sign-
   Post a stop sign on your door asking students, "Stop! Do I have my materials?"

5 Reflect & Adjust

How did the strategy go?

The BYO list seemed to really help. Students checked outside my door, and most remembered their materials. Only 3 students forgot their materials last week!

Ask the students:

They like having the visual BYO list posted in the hall because it reminds them to plan ahead & grab that stuff before coming to my class. They said they wish their other teachers would do this too!

⊗ Troubleshooting Approach

① The Problem: Name It & Reframe It

Name the problem:

Reframe the Problem:
Remember: This part shouldn't refer to the student(s)

② Match Problem with a UDL Guideline

Which one of the 9 UDL Guidelines does this most closely align with?

- [ ] Recruiting Interest
- [ ] Sustaining Effort & Persistence
- [ ] Self Regulation
- [ ] Perception
- [ ] Language & Symbols
- [ ] Comprehension
- [ ] Physical Action
- [ ] Expression & Communication
- [ ] Executive Functions

③ Narrow Guideline to UDL Checkpoint

Which checkpoint is most relevant to the problems I'm seeing in this class?

Write the checkpoint text here:

Ask the students: Is this the problem? Summarize students' responses here:

④ Find UDL-Aligned Strategies

Strategies you already know that align with your checkpoint:

1.

2.

New strategies to try:

1.

2.

⑤ Reflect & Adjust

How did the strategy go?

Ask the students:

Journey-Mapping Approach: Modifying an Existing Lesson

There is a theme park (located about 45 minutes from where I grew up) that I have attended nearly each summer for as long as I can remember. It has always been a great park with a friendly staff, clean park grounds, great rides, and affordable food. But over the last couple decades, I've seen this small park grow into a thriving organization that is proactively thinking about the needs of their customers. In 2000, the park started a new, unprecedented program that allowed all patrons to get free soft drinks all day long with a paid park admission. Self-serve soft drink huts were placed all over the park so people could just walk up, fill up their drink, then walk away. No waiting in lines. Just free, unlimited, soft drinks all day long. Other parks were dumbfounded. I can almost hear the boards of directors at other parks discussing this, "They did what? Soft drinks are our biggest money maker! One patron alone will require at least three to four drinks over the course of a day, and at $8 per soft drink, they must be out of their minds!"

My theme park, however, was thinking about this problem from the point of view of their customers rather than thinking only about their bottom line. When I've been to other parks in the past, it's been a struggle to pay for admission for our family of four and then be gouged with $8 soft drinks and $15 meals all day long. We're a family on a budget; these high prices make it really difficult to plan how much money it will actually cost to go to a theme park. So for us, attending a theme park where we don't have to pay $8 per drink to avoid dehydration is a no-brainer!

A few years later, this same theme park added free sunscreen, which they stationed in kiosks all over the park, and free parking. In recent years they have also added scannable wristbands onto which patrons can load money that they can use all over the park. This way guests can store their backpacks and purses in a secure locker and walk, unencumbered, all over. The wristbands are even waterproof, so you can use them in the water park when all you're wearing is your bathing suit!

I can't actually prove that this theme park used a journey map to come up with these ideas, but they were certainly thinking about the barriers that might be causing patrons to leave their park early or go to a different park altogether. It's almost as if the park owners sat down and said, "Okay, let's brainstorm. What are the things that stink about going to a theme park (in other words, what are the barriers?), and how can our park remove these things from the experience people have at our park (i.e., how can we design the experience to reduce or remove these barriers?)?"

As it turns out, we can have these same user-experience kinds of conversations about the design of our instruction using something called a journey map. A journey map is a visual representation of the stages users go through when interacting with a company or product. Many industries use processes like journey mapping to plan and tweak the user's experience with their products and services. They do this by creating a journey map that evaluates the effectiveness of each step in the processes associated with their company. The pages that follow will guide you through the steps of using a journey map to design and optimize instruction by considering the teaching and learning experience from the point of view of your students. I first learned about blending UDL and journey mapping from Kim Ducharme, CAST's Director of Educational User Experience Design. You can check out her free webinar on the subject at *https://www.cast.org/products-services/events/2020/08/journey-map-instructional-planning*.

You will find elementary and middle school examples of instruction designed with the Journey-Mapping approach, along with a blank template, at the end of this section and a printable blank template on the *tinyurl.com/TransformWithUDL* website.

How Journey Mapping Works

BREAK DOWN THE LESSON.

The Gist:

Start building a journey map by breaking down a lesson into small chunks or parts.

What to Do:

1. Think through the major parts of a learning experience, which might be a lesson, a lecture, a lab, or any other instructional situation.

2. Divide your lesson into four to eight main parts. This step doesn't need to be detailed; rather, it is meant to give an overview of what happens during the course of the lesson.

3. Number each of the parts and add them, in chronological order (left to right), along the top row, labeled Activities, of your Journey-Mapping Approach template.

4. Next, grab the closest straightedge and add lines all the way down the paper in between each step of your lesson. Or, if you're the kind of person who likes to throw caution to the wind, you can just freehand your lines.

Tips and Tricks:

★ When K–12 teachers are asked to draft lesson plans, the plans they create are often required to be very detailed. The Journey-Mapping approach is not quite as detailed because we are trying to get an idea of the general movements or pieces of the lesson.

★ For some, it may be easier to start by writing the different parts of the lesson, or activities, on individual sticky notes, then combining the pieces until you have about four to eight main parts. You would then number those parts and add them, chronologically, across the Activities row of the Journey-Mapping Approach template.

For Example:

Let's look at how a seventh-grade science class lab can be broken down into seven parts:

1. Students take part in a bell-ringer activity.

2. Teacher provides lab instructions and assigns groups.

3. Students collect materials and start the lab.

4. Students fill out the lab worksheet.

5. Students put materials away.

6. Students participate in a whole-class discussion.

7. Teacher assigns homework.

Journey Mapping Approach— MS: 7th Grade Science Example

Activities	1 Bell ringer quiz over lab procedures	2 Give lab instructions & put students into groups	3 Students get materials & start their circuit lab	4 After lab, students fill out lab worksheet	5 Students put materials away	6 Whole class discussion to wrap up lab	7 Assign home-work: email me typed lab worksheet
Materials							
Level of Emotion or Productivity							
Possible Barriers							
UDL-Aligned Strategies to Remove Barriers							

LIST THE MATERIALS.

The Gist:

Next, list the materials that you and the students will need for each part of the lesson.

What to Do:

1. Think through each of the parts of the lesson, or activities, and consider what materials you and the students will use.

2. Under each part of the lesson, add the materials you and the students will need for that part.

Tips and Tricks:

★ Listing the materials is important because sometimes the learning barrier has to do with access to, or familiarity with, the materials themselves.

For Example:

In our example, our science teacher has gone through each part of the lesson and has listed materials that will either be used by the students or herself.

Journey Mapping Approach– MS: 7th Grade Science Example

	1	2	3	4	5	6	7
Activities	Bell ringer quiz over lab procedures	Give lab instructions & put students into groups	Students get materials & start their circuit lab	After lab, students fill out lab worksheet	Students put materials away	Whole class discussion to wrap up lab	Assign home-work: email me typed lab worksheet
Materials	• Bell ringer slip • Pen/pencil	• Worksheets • Pen/pencil	• Switches • Batteries • Wires • Light bulbs	• Worksheets • Pen/pencil			• Worksheets • Computer • Internet access
Level of Emotion or Productivity							
Possible Barriers							
UDL-Aligned Strategies to Remove Barriers							

ASSESS STUDENT EMOTION/ENGAGEMENT/PRODUCTIVITY LEVEL.

The Gist:

Think about the lesson from the students' perspective and indicate with an X how high or low their emotion, engagement, or productivity might be for each part.

What to Do:

1. For each part of the lesson, consider your students' perspective. Choose one class period to use as your lens.

2. Once you have decided on a class period, think about how that particular group of students, as a whole, might feel about the different activities.

3. On your Journey-Mapping Approach template, indicate or predict the level of emotion, engagement, or productivity your students require for each part of the lesson.

4. Use the dotted line as your emotional baseline and mark your prediction for students' emotion, engagement, or productivity as being high (above the baseline) or low (below the baseline). The farther away from the baseline, the more intense their reactions might be.

5. Place an X somewhere on this continuum between highly engaged/ productive to less engaged/productive directly under each activity.

6. (Optional) If it aids your overall understanding of the flow of the lesson from the perspective of your students, feel free to connect the X's with a line.

Tips and Tricks:

★ Don't get too hung up on finding the perfect spot for your X. This step is really just about putting yourself in the students' shoes and considering which activities might be causing problems for them.

★ The emotion, productivity, or engagement row can be tricky because sometimes students having high emotion is good, and sometimes it's not. In other words, don't assume that a low X = bad and a high X =

good. This will, of course, depend on the nature of your lesson and instructional activities.

★ Remember that the farther away from the baseline your X is (either higher or lower), ostensibly the more intense your students' feelings are.

For Example:

In our example, the teacher has indicated that in the third part of her lesson, she will have students collect materials and start the lab. Over the last couple years, she noticed that students really enjoy this particular lab, so she decides to put an X about halfway between the baseline and the top line of the Level of Emotion or Productivity scale for the lab in part 3 of the lesson in order to signify that students' engagement with the lab activity is rather high.

Journey Mapping Approach– MS: 7th Grade Science Example

	1	2	3	4	5	6	7
Activities	Bell ringer quiz over lab procedures	Give lab instructions & put students into groups	Students get materials & start their circuit lab	After lab, students fill out lab worksheet	Students put materials away	Whole class discussion to wrap up lab	Assign homework; email me typed lab worksheet
Materials	• Bell ringer slip • Pen/pencil	• Worksheets • Pen/pencil	• Switches • Batteries • Wires • Light bulbs	• Worksheets • Pen/pencil			• Worksheets • Computer • Internet access
Level of Emotion or Productivity	X	X	X	X	X	X	X
Possible Barriers							
UDL-Aligned Strategies to Remove Barriers							

BRAINSTORM THE POSSIBLE BARRIERS.

The Gist:

As you consider each part of your lesson, begin to imagine any possible barriers students might encounter.

What to Do:

1. Reflect on each part of your lesson individually, and think about any possible barriers students might encounter.

2. In your Journey-Mapping Approach template, fill out the Possible Barriers row with two to four of the more glaring potential barriers you thought of for each part.

Tips and Tricks:

★ Don't worry, you don't have to think of every possible barrier! Instead, think of some of the bigger issues for the students in this particular group.

★ Another way to contemplate barriers is to ask yourself a couple questions: What do the students in this class/course typically struggle with? What do I receive 50 emails or questions about? Next, consider what may be causing these issues—your answer may lead you to find a significant student learning barrier.

For Example:

A teacher recalls that, in previous school years, students, although very excited and engaged about this lab, have had difficulty gathering their materials quickly and efficiently. Sometimes their heightened sense of excitement causes them to miss many of the directions, and they often forget what they're supposed to do once they start the actual lab. Additionally, this particular group of students has had difficulty with transitions, which often causes them to take longer than necessary.

For these reasons, the teacher lists the following two barriers for part 3 of her lesson:

Transitions can cause chaos.

Do they know what to do once they are in the lab?

Journey Mapping Approach— MS: 7th Grade Science Example

	1	2	3	4	5	6	7
Activities	Bell ringer quiz over lab procedures	Give lab instructions & put students into groups	Students get materials & start their circuit lab	After lab, students fill out lab worksheet	Students put materials away	Whole class discussion to wrap up lab	Assign homework: email me typed lab worksheet
Materials	• Bell ringer slip • Pen/pencil	• Worksheets • Pen/pencil	• Switches • Batteries • Wires • Light bulbs	• Worksheets • Pen/pencil			• Worksheets • Computer • Internet access
Level of Emotion or Productivity							
Possible Barriers	• Students have difficulty getting focused (after recess) • Bell work feels like busy-work	• Been sitting & listening for 15 minutes— may lose focus • Don't want to work in groups	• Transition could be chaos • Do they know what to do once they are in the lab?	• Hard to get focused after lab? • Students don't understand the worksheet?	• Transitions= chaos • They may get out of control • Could take a long time	• Will they be too high-energy? • Tchr.-focused? • Some don't like discussions	• Don't know how to type • Don't have good internet • Don't have a computer
UDL-Aligned Strategies to Remove Barriers							

DESIGN TO REMOVE BARRIERS.

The Gist:

In order to reduce any barriers to learning, turn to your UDL Guidelines and checkpoints for solutions.

What to Do:

1. It will be helpful for you to have access to a copy of the UDL Guidelines for reference during this step. You can find the UDL Guidelines in several places: 1) the appendix of this book, 2) the website that accompanies this book (*tinyurl.com/TransformWithUDL*), and 3) the CAST UDL Guidelines website (*http://udlguidelines.cast.org/*).

2. As you read one column at a time, from top to bottom, see if any new barriers jump out at you that you didn't consider in the previous step. If so, jot these down in or near the barriers box.

3. Next, look at each of the barriers you have listed for that part of the lesson. Which of these seems to be the most significant for students?

4. Choose this barrier.

5. Ask yourself, "Which one of the nine UDL Guidelines is this barrier related to?"

6. Once you determine the UDL Guideline that is most closely related, look through the checkpoints to find the one that fits with your most significant learning barrier for this part of the lesson.

7. Brainstorm some ideas or strategies that would help you reduce this barrier and add these in the bottom row labeled UDL-Aligned Strategies to Remove Barriers.

8. Follow the same instructions for each part of the lesson.

9. Finally, go back through your lesson and select one strategy to try for each of the parts of your lesson. Circle your selected strategy.

Tips and Tricks:

★ If you get stuck and can't decide which barrier is the most significant, try asking your students. Explain that you're trying to evaluate your lessons and experimenting a bit and that you need help deciding which changes are the most important; then give them some options and let them choose. In my experience, students love to make their opinions known, and you can get some valuable insight into their learning needs in the process.

For Example:

After our teacher looked at the third part of the lesson (collecting materials and starting the lab), from the top of the chart to the bottom, it occurred to her that two simple solutions could reduce the barriers of students forgetting the announcements: 1) she could provide her students with a checklist of the directions, and 2) she could presort materials into a box for each group. Both of these solutions can be associated with the Executive Functions Guideline, and the checklist directions could actually be a solution to fit all four of the Executive Functions checkpoints.

Journey Mapping Approach– MS: 7th Grade Science Example

	1	2	3	4	5	6	7
Activities	Bell ringer quiz over lab procedures	Give lab instructions & put students into groups	Students get materials & start their circuit lab	After lab, students fill out lab worksheet	Students put materials away	Whole class discussion to wrap up lab	Assign homework: email me typed lab worksheet
Materials	• Bell ringer slip • Pen/pencil	• Worksheets • Pen/pencil	• Switches • Batteries • Wires • Light bulbs	• Worksheets • Pen/pencil			• Worksheets • Computer • Internet access
Level of Emotion or Productivity							
Possible Barriers	• Students have difficulty getting focused (after recess) • Bell work feels like busy-work	• Been sitting & listening for 15 minutes– may lose focus • Don't want to work in groups	• Transition could be chaos • Do they know what to do once they are in the lab?	• Hard to get focused after lab? • Students don't understand the worksheet?	• Transitions= chaos • They may get out of control • Could take a long time	• Will they be too high-energy? • Tchr.-focused? • Some don't like discussions	• Don't know how to type • Don't have good internet • Don't have a computer
UDL-Aligned Strategies to Remove Barriers	• Mindfulness activity • Mood map • Class pencils available	• Allow students to choose to work in a group of 2-3 or individually	• Use a checklist for directions • Pre-sort materials into a box for each group	• Could the lab worksheet be a graphic organizer?	• Students leave materials in boxes at their tables (saves time & chaos)	• Use an active strategy– like snowball fight or swap meet for students to discuss	• Does this need to be typed? why? • Is this step necessary?

REFLECT AND ADJUST.

The Gist:

After you've tried out your new strategies in class, take time to reflect on how the new strategies went and decide if you want to keep them or try something different.

What to Do:

1. Think about the lesson as a whole and ask yourself the following questions:

   a. How did it go?

   b. How did students respond to the strategies I put in place?

   c. Were the learning barriers significantly reduced or did they remain unchanged?

2. Now look at each part of the lesson and the UDL-aligned strategies you used to reduce learning barriers. Did all the strategies work? If not, which ones will you keep? Which ones will you tweak? Which ones need to be replaced?

3. If you are replacing the strategy for one or more parts, consider trying one of the other items you listed but didn't initially circle in the UDL-Aligned Strategies to Remove Barriers part of your Journey-Mapping Approach template.

Tips and Tricks:

★ Solving problems in education is not always a clear-cut endeavor. The process of teaching and learning is complex, with many different factors. We're not always going to guess right the first time . . . and that's okay. Journey mapping is meant to be iterative.

For Example:

The teacher determines that she can lay out the checklist she gives students so that it solves both the problem of gathering materials and that of the students not knowing what to do in their lab groups. She adds a section at the beginning labeled Materials to Gather, which helps students quickly collect what they need so they have plenty of time to complete their lab. After the lab, she conducts an informal survey asking students what really helped them complete their lab and what she might need to reexamine for next year's class. Most groups indicate that the checklist was really helpful and that they liked being able to check off each step as they finished it. The teacher decides to use this checklist style of directions in other upcoming labs.

What follows are include two examples of lessons that have been redesigned with the Journey-Mapping approach and a blank version of the Journey-Mapping Approach template.

Journey Mapping Approach– ES: 2nd Grade Music Example

	1 Intro	2 Video	3 Dynamic Markings	4 Dynamics Flashcards	5 Singing	6 Worksheet
Activities	Teacher explains the definition of dynamics in music	Students watch a video about dynamics	Students raise hands to identify dynamic markings on cards held up by teacher	Student partners quiz each other on dynamics markings using flashcards.	As a whole class, students practice singing a song at different dynamic levels	Students match the names of dynamic markings with their symbols
Materials		• Video link • Projector • Screen • Speakers	• 1 set of dynamic marking flash-cards	• Multiple sets of dynamics marking flashcards	• 1 set of dynamic marking flash-cards	• Worksheets • Pencils
Level of Emotion or Productivity						
Possible Barriers	• This class is often high-energy when they arrive- may need to calm down • Boring intro	• Students don't usually like this video • Maybe find a different way to introduce?	• They've been sitting for a while now • May need practice with terms before being quizzed	• Students may not be able to find a partner • Do they know the info well enough for flashcards yet?	• Just singing a song over and over might get boring • If they're high energy, they may get out of hand	• Boring • Is this actually going to help them learn about how dynamics work?
UDL-Aligned Strategies to Remove Barriers	• Start with a song with motions to focus their energy • Sing the song louder and softer to introduce the concept without telling them what it is	• Move video to end? • Listen to Haydn's Surprise Symphony & use a visual listening map	Introduce terms piano & forte	Sing a familiar song- teacher holds up flashcards for p & f and students sing softer or louder to match dynamics on cards	• Play a singing game: hide an object in room & students sing louder & softer to guide a student to object	Finish with a better video and review piano & forte

Journey Mapping Approach– MS: Middle School Math Example

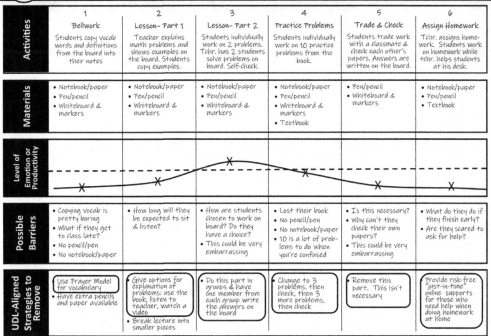

	1 Bellwork	2 Lesson– Part 1	3 Lesson– Part 2	4 Practice Problems	5 Trade & Check	6 Assign Homework
Activities	Students copy vocab words and definitions from the board into their notes	Teacher explains math problems and shows examples on the board. Students copy examples.	Students individually work on 2 problems. Tchr. has 2 students solve problems on board. Self-check.	Students individually work on 10 practice problems from the book.	Students trade work with a classmate & check each other's papers. Answers are written on the board.	Tchr. assigns homework. Students work on homework while tchr. helps students at his desk.
Materials	• Notebook/paper • Pen/pencil • Whiteboard & markers	• Notebook/paper • Pen/pencil • Whiteboard & markers	• Notebook/paper • Pen/pencil • Whiteboard & markers	• Notebook/paper • Pen/pencil • Whiteboard & markers • Textbook	• Pen/pencil • Whiteboard & markers	• Notebook/paper • Pen/pencil • Textbook
Level of Emotion or Productivity						
Possible Barriers	• Copying vocab is pretty boring • What if they get to class late? • No pencil/pen • No notebook/paper	• How long will they be expected to sit & listen?	• How are students chosen to work on board? Do they have a choice? • This could be very embarrassing	• Lost their book • No pencil/pen • No notebook/paper • 10 is a lot of problems to do when you're confused	• Is this necessary? • Why can't they check their own papers? • This could be very embarrassing	• What do they do if they finish early? • Are they scared to ask for help?
UDL-Aligned Strategies to Remove	• Use Frayer Model for vocabulary • Have extra pencils and paper available	• Give options for explanation of problems: use the book, listen to teacher, watch a video • Break lecture into smaller pieces	• Do this part in groups & have one member from each group write the answers on the board	• Change to 3 problems, then check, then 3 more problems, then check	• Remove this part. This isn't necessary	• Provide risk-free "just-in-time" online supports for those who need help when doing homework at home

Journey Mapping Approach

Activities	
Materials	
Level of Emotion or Productivity	
Possible Barriers	
UDL-Aligned Strategies to Remove Barriers	

Final Thoughts for the Journey-Mapping Approach

Before moving on to Step 6, let's take a moment to reflect on your UDL journey up to this point. You began with a basic idea of UDL, then worked through the first four steps to gain or strengthen a UDL mindset. Next, you started implementing UDL in Step 5 by exploring one or more of the three different approaches to UDL lesson design. And now you've arrived here! What a journey!

The last leg of this journey helps you move toward a place of consistent and thorough UDL implementation by encouraging you to keep working on UDL. Keep seeking out those learning barriers, keep reflecting, and keep soliciting feedback from your students!

6

Step 6: Commit to Design for Equitable Instruction

Commit to using the evidence-based planning framework of UDL to design more equitable instruction that reduces learning barriers and to continue reflecting and refining with student input.

Throughout your journey in reading and working through Steps 1–4, you've been able to examine your practice and begin to shift into a UDL mindset. In Step 5, you had the opportunity to try on UDL using one or more of the three approaches to lesson planning with UDL. Now, in Step 6, I want to invite you to commit yourself to designing for equitable instruction through UDL. This chapter is organized in two sections. The first section leads you through the process of continuing to uncover learning barriers while also reflecting on your practices and setting goals for the future. The second part gives you the opportunity to dig a little deeper into your understanding of the UDL framework through a brief overview of UDL and descriptions of how and why the 31 checkpoints that make up the UDL Guidelines and its three principles work.

Look for Learning Barriers

In Step 5 you began looking for the accidental learning barriers that sometimes show up in your instruction; we call these *instructional barriers*. Your work in the first five steps of your UDL mindset shift has given you lots of practice identifying these barriers in your classroom. Although these instructional barriers are obviously important, other types of barriers may be a little more difficult to spot. These other learning barriers fall into three categories: systemic barriers, communicative barriers, and attitudinal barriers (Ralabate & Nelson, 2017).

Brainstorm some of the systemic, communicative, and attitudinal barriers that may also show up for your students and add them to the columns here.

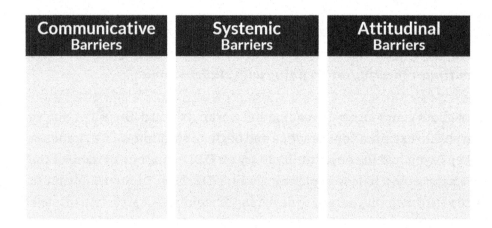

Communicative Barriers	Systemic Barriers	Attitudinal Barriers

Reflect on Your Practice

Reflection has been shown to be one of the most effective practices for teachers who want to improve their impact in the classroom, but unfortunately this critical practice often gets pushed to the back burner (and sometimes off the stove entirely) when teachers are short on time. Here are a few quick ways to build in time to reflect on your practice as you move forward on your journey toward UDL implementation.

- ★ **On Your Commute Home:** Use voice notes or type yourself a message that examines the pain points and the wins from your lessons that day or week.

- ★ **Sticky-Note Reminders:** Add sticky notes or comments to the space where you keep your lesson plans (plan book, digital calendar, Google Classroom, etc.) to remind yourself of what worked well, what you'd like to change, and what you might need to research for the next time you teach this lesson. Begin the practice of pulling out your old plans and looking at your notes to self from the last time you taught that lesson.

- ★ **Hashtags:** Use Twitter or another social media platform to have virtual conversations with educators across the globe. Share your wins and pain points and look for ideas from others.

Solicit Feedback From Your Students

One of the quickest ways to find the barriers that hold back your students is to ask the students themselves! Students really appreciate being asked to participate in their own learning, and we build our trust with them when we listen and make changes based on their input. Here are a few simple ways to solicit feedback from students.

- ★ **Happys & Crappys** (aka Roses & Thorns): At the end of the week, have students report (on sticky notes, via Google Forms, etc.) on one thing they feel like they really understood or enjoyed that week and on one thing they're still confused about or didn't like. Remind them to be honest, but kind, and if you make changes based on their ideas, let them know!

- ★ **Focus Group:** Ask a fellow teacher, an instructional coach, or a non-evaluating administrator to do a focus group with your class to determine what things are really helping them learn and what changes they suggest you could make to improve their learning. In this situation, you would leave the room for 10–15 minutes, and the fellow teacher, instructional coach, or non-evaluating administrator would ask students the following two questions, collect their ideas, and report back to you (in a general way) about what the students shared:

1. What things are helping you learn in this class?

2. What changes do you suggest for the teacher that could improve your learning?

Make a Plan

Make a plan for how you will . . .

Continue to seek out and reduce learning barriers:

_____

_____

_____

_____

Reflect on your practice:

_____

_____

_____

_____

Solicit feedback from students:

_____

_____

_____

_____

Set *One* Goal for UDL Implementation

What goal do I want to accomplish by using UDL in my classroom?

_____

_____

_____

_____

How will I know when I've accomplished this goal? What evidence will I need to prove to myself that the goal has been achieved?

_____

_____

_____

_____

What is a reasonable timeline for accomplishing this goal?

_____

_____

_____

_____

How can I break this goal into smaller milestones?

_____

_____

_____

_____

Set a Time for Reflection

When would you like to do a check-in to see where you are in meeting your goals? It may be helpful to actually add an appointment in your paper or digital calendar to remind yourself to return to this page.

Did you meet the goal you set for yourself?

If *yes*, how did it go?

_____

_____

_____

_____

_____

If *no*, what resources do you need in order to meet your goal?

_____

_____

_____

A Quick Review of UDL Principles and Guidelines

Part of committing yourself to being a UDL practitioner is really digging into the UDL framework itself. When I first started learning about UDL, my mindset shift occurred pretty quickly, but I felt overwhelmed with the awareness of just how much I *didn't* know about UDL! So, I began reading every UDL book I could find and attending every UDL Twitter chat and webinar that I saw online. But it wasn't until I'd taken the time to read through and learn about each of the three principles, the nine guidelines, and the 31 checkpoints that I felt like I truly understood UDL. The following section contains a brief description of each of the 31 UDL checkpoints, and in part 3 of this book, you will find strategies aligned to each of these. You can also explore the CAST UDL Guidelines website to discover the multitude of research studies and articles that support each of the checkpoints.

NOTE: You may have wondered why the CAST UDL framework starts with Recruiting Interest as guideline number 7 instead of starting with number 1, and you wouldn't be alone in your wonderings! In earlier iterations of the framework, the left-to-right order was different than it is in the current version of the UDL Guidelines. The first couple of versions had Representation (shown in purple) on the left, Action & Expression (shown in blue) in the middle, and Engagement (shown in green) on the right. Some UDL practitioners argued that Engagement should be placed to the left side to indicate that it is of equal importance and that the UDL Guidelines do not need to be applied in any particular sequence. If it were on the left side, that would put it first in the left-to-right reading order of the English language. These UDLers posited that if students aren't engaged, then the rest of the framework doesn't do much good! So, in the next revamp of the UDL Guidelines, the Engagement column was moved to the left side, but the numbers remained the same. For more information on the structure of the CAST UDL Guidelines, visit *https://udlguidelines.cast.org/more/about-graphic-organizer*.

Using the Affective Network to Improve and Deepen Learner Motivation

Principle 1: Provide Multiple Means of Engagement

▶ Recruiting Interest

  ▶ 7.1: Optimize individual choice and autonomy

  ▶ 7.2: Optimize relevance, value, and authenticity

  ▶ 7.3: Minimize threats and distractions

- ▶ Sustaining Effort & Persistence
  - ▶ 8.1: Heighten salience of goals and objectives
  - ▶ 8.2: Vary demands and resources to optimize challenge
  - ▶ 8.3: Foster collaboration and community
  - ▶ 8.4: Increase mastery-oriented feedback
- ▶ Self Regulation
  - ▶ 9.1: Promote expectations and beliefs that optimize motivation
  - ▶ 9.2: Facilitate personal coping strategies
  - ▶ 9.3: Develop self-assessment and reflection

Okay, let's talk candidly for a moment . . . teacher to teacher. Our students are bored. Not all of them, of course, but I'd venture to say that a fair number are. Many of our K–12 students sit in chairs attached to desks, listening or filling out packets of worksheets, not talking to or interacting with their peers, for hours and hours at a time. Have you tried this as an adult? Sitting for three to six hours listening to someone else talk about something you don't feel a connection to, without the ability to interact with the people around you or get up and stretch? Maybe at a conference or at a professional development workshop? I mean, yes, you get up and change locations, but for the most part, you're sitting and listening all day long.

It's the WORST! I can't sustain this for 45 minutes, let alone for six hours. I get restless and irritable, and I start looking for any reason to escape, if only for a few minutes:

- ★ "Um . . . a pressing email just came in; I need to go take care of some things."

- ★ "My blood sugar is starting to drop; I need to go get something to eat real quick."

- ★ "I think I had too much coffee this morning; I need to go use the restroom."

- ★ "Oh, shoot *(looking at phone)!* It's my kid's school calling. I better take this."

It should be noted that I'm a rule-follower, and I'm generally compliant in a teaching and learning situation, so I probably wouldn't cause problems or disruptions. But I can definitely see how and why some of our students would.

Now, obviously I'm not talking about students sitting in *your* classroom, I'm talking about *other* teachers' classrooms. But I think we have all been in this situation, and hopefully we can all recognize that it's not fun, and it's generally not very conducive to learning. The following sections of this chapter will explore the three UDL Guidelines that address engagement: Recruiting Interest, Sustaining Effort & Persistence, and Self Regulation. As you proceed through this and later chapters, please feel free to highlight, underline, dog-ear, and add pictures in any way that helps you process the information.

Recruiting Interest (7)

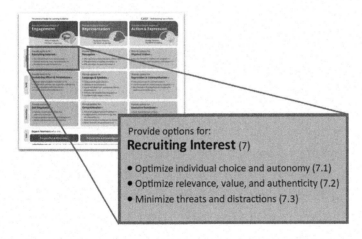

Provide options for:
Recruiting Interest (7)

- Optimize individual choice and autonomy (7.1)
- Optimize relevance, value, and authenticity (7.2)
- Minimize threats and distractions (7.3)

OPTIMIZE INDIVIDUAL CHOICE AND AUTONOMY (7.1)

Offering students choice is crucial to recruiting their interest and increasing their engagement. In fact, a quick glance at the UDL framework will show you that each of the nine UDL Guidelines is also tied to the idea of student choice. Educators are asked to "provide options for" each of the guidelines. Provide options for comprehension, provide options for expression and communication, provide options for self-regulation, and so on. If you are new to UDL and you are looking for a first step, a way to dip your toe in the pool of UDL, I suggest starting by offering your students choices.

OPTIMIZE RELEVANCE, VALUE, AND AUTHENTICITY (7.2)

The engagement principle of UDL is all about the *why* of learning because our brains are designed to look for connections to new information. All day long, humans receive sensory information from what we hear, see, taste, smell, and feel. But our brains can't focus on every stimulant, so they sort through the stimuli and decide which ones are given priority and which are ignored. Like familiarity-seeking missiles, our brains tend to remember information that has an emotional resonance or connection. So the more we can tie content to topics and material that are relevant to students, the more engaged they will be.

MINIMIZE THREATS AND DISTRACTIONS (7.3)

In her 2019 book, *Engage the Brain*, UDL expert Allison Posey explains research that has shown us just how real these threats can be for the students experiencing them. She highlights one study that shows that some students have the same physiological responses (raised pulse, increased sweat, etc.) to public speaking or reading aloud in class as someone would have if they were being chased by a tiger! I don't know about you, but I'm not going to be focusing on trigonometry if I'm face to face with a real or metaphorical tiger. In the epic battle of trig versus tiger, tiger always wins. So, when our students experience threats in the classroom setting, they are less likely to be able to concentrate on the teaching and learning that are taking place. The good news is that we, as teachers, can make simple changes to our instruction to ameliorate these threats and distractions for our students.

Sustaining Effort & Persistence (8)

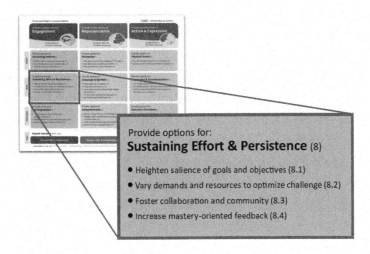

Provide options for:
Sustaining Effort & Persistence (8)

- Heighten salience of goals and objectives (8.1)
- Vary demands and resources to optimize challenge (8.2)
- Foster collaboration and community (8.3)
- Increase mastery-oriented feedback (8.4)

HEIGHTEN SALIENCE OF GOALS AND OBJECTIVES (8.1)

When travelling, my family and I typically use a GPS or a map application on one of our smartphones. First, we type in where we're starting and plug in the destination, and then we're suddenly provided with many different choices: routes, tolls versus no tolls, form of transportation, and so on. As it turns out, when we know where we're going (the goal), we can get there in lots of different ways (the options). We can think of teaching and learning in much the same way. When we know where our students are and we know what we want them to learn, the route they take can be more flexible depending on the specific learning needs of each individual student. A rather unfortunate saying I've heard in Kentucky that sums up this point quite succinctly is "There's more than one way to skin a cat." This UDL checkpoint, *8.1: Heighten salience of goals and objectives*, suggests that we should elevate the importance or prominence of goals in our classroom so that flexible learning options can be measured against their ability to help students attain the goal.

VARY DEMANDS AND RESOURCES TO OPTIMIZE CHALLENGE (8.2)

In order to help our students sustain effort and develop persistence, we can include tools to vary demands and resources to optimize challenge. Are students tired of writing in their journals? Vary the resources by having them write on their desks with dry-erase markers and taking a picture. Do some of your students tune out during class discussions? Vary the demand by having them record their discussion response as a video or audio file. Are they still doing the work? Yes. Are they still meeting the standards or student learning objectives? You bet! This UDL checkpoint, *8.2: Vary demands and resources to optimize challenge*, can also be applied when you consider how to challenge high-achieving learners. Perhaps they've already mastered the content you planned to teach for the next three days. How do you still give them learning opportunities without simply asking them to do *more* problems or answer *more* questions? One strategy is to plan instruction for the highest-achieving learners but provide scaffolding and supports for all students (learn more about this strategy, called *Teaching Up*, on the *tinyurl.com/TransformWithUDL* website).

FOSTER COLLABORATION AND COMMUNITY (8.3)

If you've ever worked in a dysfunctional group setting, you've probably experienced many of the same troubles that students encounter when they try to figure out how to function as a cohesive unit for group work. In my own experience, I've found that when group work is unstructured, the members spend a great deal of time and effort trying to ascertain the answers to several logistical questions instead of working on the task at hand. Without proper guidance and expectations, these groups can end in frustration and with subpar finished products. Luckily, teachers can do some simple things to set their student groups up for success. When planning group work of any kind (group projects, group brainstorming, peer feedback groups, etc.), it helps to keep the questions in the following table in mind. You can then use these common questions to proactively plan for student collaboration by making sure you provide access to the following information (preferably in a version they can continue to return to for reference).

	POSSIBLE STUDENT QUESTIONS	INFORMATION YOU CAN PROACTIVELY PROVIDE
WHY?	• Why are we doing this project? • Why do we have to work in groups?	• Connect to learning objectives. • Written explanation of why group work is essential
WHO?	• Who is responsible for what? • Who do we go to when we need help?	• Roles • Help
WHAT?	• What are we supposed to be doing? • What does a good example look like?	• Instructions • Examples
WHEN?	• When is this due? • How do we know if we're where we should be timewise?	• Due dates • Check-in points
HOW?	• How are we supposed to present this? • How do we know if we're doing it right?	• Finished product • Rubric

Another aspect of group work that can be tricky is how to form the actual groups. On one hand, you may want students to be able to work with their friends so they feel comfortable and confident, but on the other, you may want to make sure the highly compliant students don't all form one group while all the disengaged students form another. Luckily, some interesting ways to group students allow them both to step outside their comfort zone and work in groups with students outside their friend group, while also giving them the autonomy to have some aspect of choice in their groups (see checkpoint 8.3 in part 3 of this book for some grouping ideas).

INCREASE MASTERY-ORIENTED FEEDBACK (8.4)

Mastery-oriented feedback is less about compliance or "doing it perfectly" and more about encouraging students to progress toward mastery. It's less about how many questions students got wrong and more about figuring out why they got those answers wrong. A major barrier to providing mastery-oriented feedback is that it can be very time-consuming. If a middle school teacher sees 150–200 students in a given week, it's almost impossible to provide detailed feedback for each student on each assignment. But let's consider the text of this particular checkpoint. UDL checkpoint 8.4 asks educators to *increase* mastery-oriented feedback. It doesn't ask educators to *only* use mastery-oriented feedback. That's just not a reasonable request in every teaching and learning situation. As with all UDL, integrating the framework works much better when teachers make one small change at a time. So, instead of going from a 50-question multiple-choice test to a 10-question essay test (which may provide more options for offering mastery-oriented feedback), an instructor could start with a 40-question multiple-choice exam, with one 10-point essay.

Self Regulation (9)

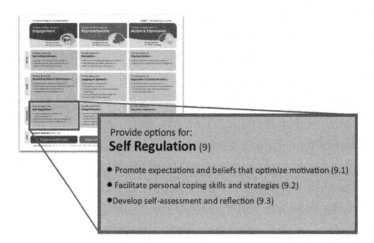

PROMOTE EXPECTATIONS AND BELIEFS THAT OPTIMIZE MOTIVATION (9.1)

If I were teaching a class on making delicious sandwiches, I might assign the following project: "For your assignment, you will make and submit a correctly made PB&J sandwich." So, when I sit down to grade my students' peanut butter and jelly sandwiches, I have what I consider to be a "correct" PB&J in mind: honey-wheat bread with smooth peanut butter and straw-berry jelly. There should be slightly more peanut butter than jelly, and also, the sandwich must be sliced diagonally. Is that what you were thinking when you first read "make and submit a correctly made PB&J sandwich"? Maybe. But maybe not. All too often, teachers unintentionally ask students to read their minds, and then they're surprised and even disappointed when the students don't turn in the work they want. This checkpoint, *9.1: Promote expectations and beliefs that optimize motivation*, asks educators to be explicit in their instructions and expectations. Being explicit in expec-tations means that, as teachers, we shouldn't assume our students know what we expect of them; rather, we should tell them exactly what we want.

FACILITATE PERSONAL COPING SKILLS AND STRATEGIES (9.2)

One thing I've always struggled with (that most other adults seem to be able to do easily) is sitting still in church. I remember getting in trouble as a pre-teen for loudly folding origami frogs and flowers out of the church bulletin during the sermon. When I was a teenager, the other youth and I would get angry looks because we kept giggling at the risqué language in the bible's Song of Solomon. During college, when I came home on the weekends to visit, I would amuse myself during church by labeling the chord progres-sions in the hymnal (former music majors may remember this tedious exercise from their music theory courses). I always got the impression that what I was doing (origami, giggling at Song of Solomon, and labeling chord progressions) meant that I was immature, but in fact, I was employing coping strategies that would enable me to be able to sit for long periods of time. Full disclosure: Now I'm in my 40s, and I still take knitting or crochet-ing to church with me so I can sit and listen to the sermon.

Coping skills and strategies are very important, especially for students who struggle with attention, organization, memory, and other executive functioning skills. Humans aren't born with these coping skills and strategies; they have to learn them. Educators can help students evaluate their need and use of coping skills and strategies in a number of ways.

DEVELOP SELF-ASSESSMENT AND REFLECTION (9.3)

Human brains are wired for setting and achieving goals. This is part of the reason that checklists can be so motivating. However, if we don't take time to reflect and assess ourselves, we may not know where we are starting or where we are going. Some students may arrive in your classroom with these skills already, but many will not have fully developed these valuable self-regulation skills. Rather than passing the buck (i.e., passing the responsibility) along to the next educator, we have the power to begin cultivating these skills in our students today, no matter where they are on the path to self-assessment.

Using the Recognition Network to Improve Student Understanding and Retention

UDL Principle 2: Provide Multiple Means of Representation

- ► Perception
  - ► 1.1: Offer ways of customizing the display of information
  - ► 1.2: Offer alternatives for auditory information
  - ► 1.3: Offer alternatives for visual information
- ► Language & Symbols
  - ► 2.1: Clarify vocabulary and symbols
  - ► 2.2: Clarify syntax and structure

- ▶ 2.3: Support decoding of text, mathematical notation, and symbols

- ▶ 2.4: Promote understanding across languages

- ▶ 2.5: Illustrate through multiple media

- ▶ Comprehension

  - ▶ 3.1: Activate or supply background knowledge

  - ▶ 3.2: Highlight patterns, critical features, big ideas, and relationships

  - ▶ 3.3: Guide information processing and visualization

  - ▶ 3.4: Maximize transfer and generalization

In the fall of 2020 at the University of Kentucky, my office, the Center for the Enhancement of Learning and Teaching (CELT), and the P20 Motivation and Learning Lab conducted a large-scale research study under the expert direction of Ellen Usher, educational psychology professor, and Kathi Kern, history professor and then director of CELT. This study, named the TLC (Teaching and Learning during COVID-19) Study, surveyed over 7,000 undergraduate students and 111 instructors to seek understanding of the complex nature of postsecondary education in the midst of a global pandemic. One of the incentives for instructors who encouraged students to take the survey was that the research team would report back some of their preliminary findings and would continue to do so as the data analysis continued.

As someone who emails and communicates with higher education instructors on a regular basis, I know that these educators (not unlike their K–12 counterparts) are notoriously short on time. While I'm sure these 111 instructors would have fully intended to read any academic papers our research group may have created, my gut tells me that they may not have had the time to process a dense, text-based representation of our findings while simultaneously teaching, researching, answering emails, and adapting their courses to an online modality. So, our research group decided that instead of presenting the preliminary data in an academic paper, we wanted to present the findings in the form of simple one-page infographics. We created some infographics that are aimed at instructors themselves and others that are designed so instructors can give them to their students. When we introduced the infographics to a group of academic deans, they were really excited about sharing the information with their colleagues and students, and they especially appreciated the easily digestible format of the infographics. Here's an example:

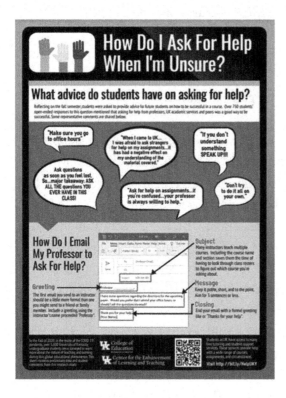

You see, I knew that using a more visual representation (an infographic) of the preliminary data would be beneficial. Not because I am a genius, but because the UDL Guidelines tell me that the way information is represented is often equally as important as the information itself.

In the United States, the form of representation that dominates education is text. Reading and writing are fundamental to the day-to-day operations of most schools in America. Those students who excel in text-based areas tend to perform better than students who struggle with reading and writing. However, many of the founders of educational philosophies, like William James and John Dewey, made it clear that all of our senses are employed in our cognitive processes. The UDL framework suggests that educators find ways to provide students with multiple means of representation and support the brain's recognition networks through perception, language and symbols, and comprehension.

Perception (1)

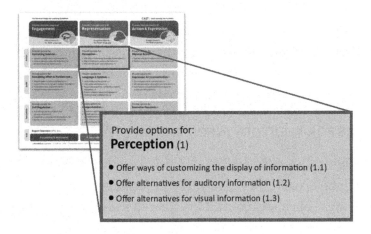

Provide options for:
Perception (1)
- Offer ways of customizing the display of information (1.1)
- Offer alternatives for auditory information (1.2)
- Offer alternatives for visual information (1.3)

OFFER WAYS OF CUSTOMIZING THE DISPLAY OF INFORMATION (1.1)

Over the last five years, I've gone from having perfect vision (never having needed glasses or contacts) to now having to hold my phone about 2 feet away from my face in order to read the print. I'm in my early 40s, so this kind of thing is to be expected, but it's still frustrating when I'm in a situation in which I encounter small print that I can't read without squinting. Now, when I eat at restaurants that have dinner lighting (anyone who's ever worked in restaurants can probably recall that moment around 5:00 when the lights go from lunch lighting to a much darker dinner lighting), I have such a hard time reading the menu that I end up using the flashlight and the magnifier on my phone to see, much to the chagrin of my teenaged daughters. Thank goodness for the built-in accessibility features that allow me to adjust the size and brightness on my phone so I can read the menu! Universal design for the win!

One important thing to remember is that simply providing students with customizable displays of information isn't enough. Some students don't even know that these customizable display features exist! Taking a few minutes at a couple points during the first months of school to teach students how and when to change the display of information can pay dividends for the rest of the year. Students who are disabled and nondisabled may need to be taught and reminded about things like increasing the font size if you're tired or adjusting to a dark background with lighter text in the evenings as ways to support learning. This checkpoint, *1.1: Offer ways of customizing the display of information*, suggests that in order to meet the needs of all learners, teachers should attempt to provide information in formats that can be adjusted according to each student's needs.

OFFER ALTERNATIVES FOR AUDITORY INFORMATION (1.2)

Some students are able to process spoken directions and information easily, but many students struggle when they hear information presented only in an auditory mode. This checkpoint, *1.2: Offer alternatives for auditory information*, suggests that if educators are going to present information auditorily, they should also accompany that spoken information with another modality.

OFFER ALTERNATIVES FOR VISUAL INFORMATION (1.3)

When information is only presented in the visual format, educators unintentionally create barriers for some students. Students with visual impairments, dyslexia, and other text-based disabilities are at a marked disadvantage when they only receive information through the use of visually presented content. This checkpoint, *1.3: Offer alternatives for visual information*, suggests that educators should find additional ways to present content, and offer these alternatives to all students, even if they don't have an Individualized Education Plan (IEP).

Language & Symbols (2)

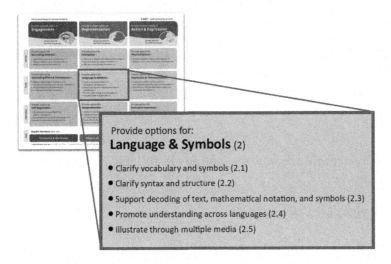

Provide options for:
Language & Symbols (2)

- Clarify vocabulary and symbols (2.1)
- Clarify syntax and structure (2.2)
- Support decoding of text, mathematical notation, and symbols (2.3)
- Promote understanding across languages (2.4)
- Illustrate through multiple media (2.5)

CLARIFY VOCABULARY AND SYMBOLS (2.1)

If you've ever attended a workshop or conference session (outside your field of expertise) where the presenter used tons of jargon, vocabulary, and field-specific language, you may have felt the frustration that this checkpoint addresses. Checkpoint *2.1: Clarify vocabulary and symbols* asks educators to explain any vocabulary, symbols, terminology, and acronyms they may use in their teaching, regardless of whether they think students know the meaning or not. Additionally, even if they have come across the terminology before, keep in mind that if they haven't heard it in a while, they may need a quick refresher. Taking a moment or two to clarify vocabulary and symbols can mean the difference between students learning the content or not learning it.

CLARIFY SYNTAX AND STRUCTURE (2.2)

According to the CAST UDL Guidelines website, *udlguidelines.cast.org*, "When the syntax of a sentence or the structure of a graphical representation is not obvious or familiar to learners, comprehension suffers." Educators can reduce the learning barriers that may exist as a result of the lack of familiarity with syntax and structure by making the relationship between components explicit.

SUPPORT DECODING OF TEXT, MATHEMATICAL NOTATION, AND SYMBOLS (2.3)

Here's a fun activity that may reveal some insights about your age and/or your past experiences:

> *What is this symbol?*
>
> #

Depending on my experience, my age, and my familiarity with the subject, this could be a

★ **Number sign:** as in "We're #1!"

★ **Sharp symbol:** as in "This is in the key of C#."

★ **Hashtag:** as in "She is a total #UDLrockstar."

★ **A pound symbol:** as in "Enter your ID, then press pound (#)."

As educators, we can't assume that our students are coming from the same experiences, age, and familiarity with the subject as we are. This means that our students may not know that certain words, notations, and symbols have different meaning in different contexts.

One of my favorite stories of this playing out in real life is a meme I've seen in multiple formats in which a young adult sends a text message to their parent, telling them something really sad, and the parent, thinking they were typing the text abbreviation for "lots of love," texts back to their young adult child, LOL.

Unfortunately for the parent in this meme, LOL, in text-speak, means "laugh out loud." So, the parent who thought they were replying "lots of love" to their young adult child's text about their dog being put to sleep, looked, to the child, like the parent was laughing out loud at the fact that their child's pet died.

Although this is a comical meme showing a classic miscommunication, it's not as funny when the misunderstanding causes students to become confused, frustrated, and lost when it applies to their schoolwork. Checkpoint *2.3: Support decoding of text, mathematical notation, and symbols* asks teachers to explain the meaning of symbols, no matter how common or well-known they are.

PROMOTE UNDERSTANDING ACROSS LANGUAGES (2.4)

The small town in Kentucky where I live happens to have a rather large population of deaf citizens. As a result, many of the public events I attend provide a sign language interpreter. One church in our town has three different church members who regularly serve as sign language interpreters for our service, and several more who are able and willing to interpret in a pinch. Many of the family events in the local school district have a sign language interpreter, including performances, awards nights, and freshman orientation. The local high school now offers students the option of American Sign Language (ASL) to fulfill their foreign language requirement. It's very cool to live in a city that keeps issues of accessibility for its deaf and hearing-impaired citizens as a top priority.

This checkpoint, *2.4: Promote understanding across languages*, asks teachers to consider the variety of students' linguistic backgrounds and proficiencies and make connections to other languages during instruction.

ILLUSTRATE THROUGH MULTIPLE MEDIA (2.5)

This checkpoint, *2.5: Illustrate through multiple media*, makes the list of my top five favorite UDL checkpoints. In many teaching and learning scenarios, information is presented in one way only, or through one medium. I like to think of this as a freeway or highway system. When information is only presented in one way, that is like having only one entrance ramp onto a major freeway. Can you imagine? This would be chaos and would likely cause a major delay in traffic. This UDL checkpoint asks educators to offer students multiple on-ramps to the information using multiple formats or media.

One easy way to remember to illustrate content through multiple media is by using the acronym MARSH. When considering how to deliver content, an educator should ask themselves how they can give students several different on-ramps to the information by giving students multiple opportunities to

★ **M**: Make it

★ **A**: Act on it

★ **R**: Read it

★ **S**: See it

★ **H**: Hear it

Now, let me be clear. I'm not implying that for every lesson, every class, every day, teachers should do all of these things, all the time. That's not realistic, and frankly, no one can sustain that much work for very long! However, it can be helpful to ask yourself, "How many of these five media did I use to teach this content, and is it possible to add just one more option?" Here are some examples:

★ How can I give them a way to *make* something creative in association with this content?

★ Can I get them up out of their seats, doing something *active* as they learn?

★ Do I always have students *read* about content?

★ Have I given them a chance to *see* what this looks like?

★ Do they have the option to *hear* or talk about this content in some way?

Comprehension (3)

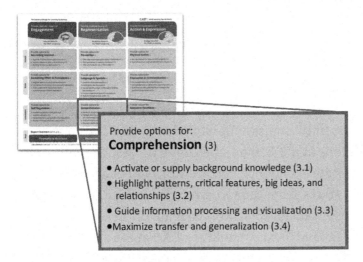

Provide options for:
Comprehension (3)

- Activate or supply background knowledge (3.1)
- Highlight patterns, critical features, big ideas, and relationships (3.2)
- Guide information processing and visualization (3.3)
- Maximize transfer and generalization (3.4)

ACTIVATE OR SUPPLY BACKGROUND KNOWLEDGE (3.1)

Students can learn content one year, then completely forget it by the time the next school year or semester rolls around. But in many cases, the content isn't gone forever, it just needs to be retrieved from their long-term, or stored, memory and pulled into their short-term, or working, memory so students can apply their background knowledge to the new content they are learning in class. Unfortunately, some teachers forget this important step, and students struggle to understand.

This checkpoint, *3.1: Activate or supply background knowledge*, reminds educators of the importance of reviewing the prerequisite knowledge before diving right into the new content. This equitable teaching practice aids in overall comprehension by removing barriers for students who may have forgotten, missed, or never learned the prior knowledge.

HIGHLIGHT PATTERNS, CRITICAL FEATURES, BIG IDEAS, AND RELATIONSHIPS (3.2)

Some of our students seem to have an innate ability to take a step back from content and pull out the big ideas and critical features, while others get bogged down and overwhelmed with all the details, consequently missing the patterns and main ideas altogether. Teachers can foster understanding and help students weed out the secondary information by following checkpoint *3.2: Highlight patterns, critical features, big ideas, and relationships.*

GUIDE INFORMATION PROCESSING AND VISUALIZATION (3.3)

For some reason, I used to always get several states in the middle of the U.S. mixed up. That is, until one fateful day when I was introduced to Chef MIMAL. Take a look at a U.S. map. Chef MIMAL stands right in the middle of the United States, and once you see him, you can't unsee him! Chef MIMAL's profile starts, from the top, with his chef hat, which is the state of Minnesota. His head and torso are made up of the states of Iowa and Missouri, and his legs and feet are made up of Arkansas and Louisiana. So, if you look at him from top to bottom, he spells the name MIMAL: Minnesota, Iowa, Missouri, Arkansas, and Louisiana. Now, using this simple visual cue and mnemonic device, I never mix up Arkansas with Missouri or Iowa with Nebraska. I've even seen a few other states added to the mix where Chef MIMAL is holding his Tennessee tray, in which he is cooking Kentucky Fried Chicken, and behind him, it seems Chef MIMAL has laid his Oklahoma-shaped butcher knife on his Texas table.

Meet Chef MIMAL

Although this example is somewhat elementary, the same ideas can be applied to information at all levels. I'll never forget learning to identify classical music in college as I prepared for the so-called drop-the-needle tests in my music history course. My friends and I made up little rhymes and lyrics to go with as many songs as we could. Two of my favorite were singing the words, "Italian, Italian, by Mendelssohn" to remember that the *Italian Symphony* was written by Felix Mendelssohn, and the words, "this is a symphony, a symphony that isn't done" to remember the tune for Franz Schubert's *Unfinished Symphony*.

According to Allison Posey, our brains are wired to remember things that are interesting or unique: "From a neurological perspective, novelty attracts attention" (p.86). So, using strategies, like the mnemonic device and visual cues to identify the states in Chef MIMAL or adding silly lyrics to classical tunes to remember composers, will help students more efficiently learn information, but it will also help them to recall this information for much longer.

MAXIMIZE TRANSFER AND GENERALIZATION (3.4)

Some of the content we teach is specific to our subject, but in order to become expert learners, our students will require additional skills that can be transferred to other fields and content areas. Unfortunately, some educators don't feel that they have the time or the academic freedom to teach things like study skills, organization, research methods, academic reading skills, and writing techniques. But these skills are absolutely necessary to create students who are flexible and can adapt to new learning situations with ease and confidence. This checkpoint, *3.4: Maximize transfer and generalization*, asks teachers to find ways to build these otherwise implicit skills into their assignments, activities, and grading.

Using the Strategic Network to Guide and Enhance Learning

UDL Principle 3: Provide Multiple Means of Action & Expression

- ▶ Physical Action

  - ▶ 4.1: Vary the methods for response and navigation

  - ▶ 4.2: Optimize access to tools and assistive technologies

- ▶ Expression & Communication

  - ▶ 5.1: Use multiple media for communication

  - ▶ 5.2: Use multiple tools for construction and composition

  - ▶ 5.3: Build fluencies with graduated levels of support for practice and performance

- ▶ Executive Functions

  - ▶ 6.1: Guide appropriate goal setting

  - ▶ 6.2: Support planning and strategy development

  - ▶ 6.3: Facilitate managing information and resources

  - ▶ 6.4: Enhance capacity for monitoring progress

The principle of *Action & Expression* is often described as being the part of UDL that deals with assessment, and while that is true, this rich principle encompasses much more than simply offering choices for assignments. The strategic networks in the brain are responsible for helping us figure out *how* to learn: 1) how to take actions that lead to learning, 2) how to express ourselves and communicate with others, and 3) how to regulate and organize ourselves for optimal learning. Understanding, and effectively using, this principle in your classroom can make a huge difference for students because giving students multiple ways to show what they know and multiple ways to interact with the content validates the variety of learners and learning needs in our classrooms. Each of the three UDL Guidelines within the Action & Expression principle (Physical Action, Expression & Communication, and Executive Functions) has its own role to play in removing learning barriers for students.

A quote often attributed to Albert Einstein (although no physical record of Einstein saying this has been found) reads, "Everyone is a genius. But if you judge a fish by its ability to climb a tree, it will live its whole life believing that it is stupid." Earlier, we talked briefly about the text-based nature of how information is represented in education. However, assessment in education is also dominated by text-based methods like writing papers and taking tests. These methods, although fairly easy to grade, don't always present an accurate representation of what students have actually learned.

My favorite guideline is the one on executive functions (you know you're a UDL nerd when you have a favorite guideline). This is important to me because teachers of students with specific learning disabilities can transform students' lives when they explicitly teach them executive functioning skills. In fact, at the school where I taught, students had a class period called Success, which was dedicated to teaching things like organization, time management, study skills, and goal setting.

In order for students to become strategic and goal-oriented expert learners, we must provide them with options for physical action, options for expression and communication, and options for executive functions. The section that follows will provide you with a brief description of each checkpoint that will help you begin to strengthen students' strategic networks through the principle of *Action & Expression*.

Physical Action (4)

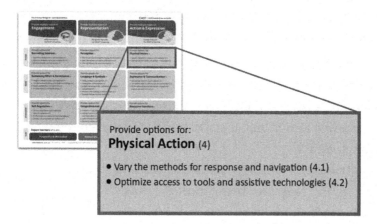

Provide options for:
Physical Action (4)

- Vary the methods for response and navigation (4.1)
- Optimize access to tools and assistive technologies (4.2)

VARY THE METHODS FOR RESPONSE AND NAVIGATION (4.1)

The first checkpoint, *4.1: Vary the methods for response and navigation*, reminds teachers of the concept of *neurovariability*. Because we know that each brain is unique, we can assume that the variety of students in our classroom will have unique ways of accessing and interacting with content. When we give students only one way to access, work with, and demonstrate understanding of content, we unintentionally place barriers in front of some of them. Varying the methods for response and navigation will help us reduce these barriers for our students and increase their chances of learning and retaining content.

OPTIMIZE ACCESS TO TOOLS AND ASSISTIVE TECHNOLOGIES (4.2)

Although it is true that the prevalence of smartphone devices has put assistive technology in the hands of many, our students may not be aware that such tools exist, much less know how to use them. As educators, we can help reduce these learning barriers for some of our students by demonstrating these assistive technologies and by providing tools that help students succeed.

Expression & Communication (5)

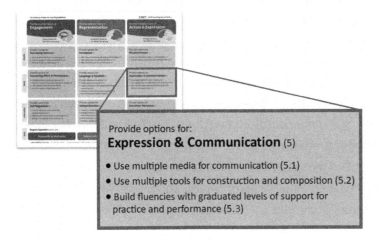

Provide options for:
Expression & Communication (5)

- Use multiple media for communication (5.1)
- Use multiple tools for construction and composition (5.2)
- Build fluencies with graduated levels of support for practice and performance (5.3)

USE MULTIPLE MEDIA FOR COMMUNICATION (5.1)

Today, the word *media* is used in many ways—social media, media centers, media player, and multimedia are just a few of the ways this word has become ubiquitous in our world. When some educators refer to creating a "multimedia" assignment or a "multimedia lesson," they typically mean they are creating assignments and lessons that are infused with technological aspects, most often video and audio components. Despite the complex modern use of the word, the term *media*, the plural form of the word *medium*, simply means "a channel or system of communication" according to the dictionary. While *media* can refer to ways of communication involving technology, the term certainly doesn't have to include technology. I say this because UDL is sometimes viewed as being synonymous with assistive technology. I'm here to tell you that while technology can be a part of implementing UDL, there are tons of highly effective low-tech and no-tech means of designing and optimizing teaching and learning in your classrooms.

If we temporarily substitute the word *media* with the word *ways*, this checkpoint, *5.1: Use multiple media for communication*, simply means, "use multiple ways to communicate." So, if lecture is your main mode of communicating content to your students, checkpoint 5.1 asks you to consider adding some other ways. This could be in the form of slide presentations, captions, video clips, graphic organizers, a sign-language interpreter, images, podcasts, and so on.

It also helps to consider how students will communicate with each other. As I've said before, not all students will be comfortable raising their hands or participating in a class discussion. This checkpoint asks us to give students multiple ways to communicate with each other—through a class discussion, a chat box, a poster paper, index cards, a Google Doc, sticky notes, and so on. But before you panic, please remember, you don't have to do *all the things* today. The Plus-One approach shows us a way to simply add one thing at a time. For more information on the Plus-One approach, refer to Chapter 5.

USE MULTIPLE TOOLS FOR CONSTRUCTION AND COMPOSITION (5.2)

On the CAST UDL Guidelines web page, *udlguidelines.cast.org*, the description of this checkpoint is so strong that I share it here as a way to introduce it:

> There is a tendency in schooling to focus on traditional tools rather than contemporary ones. This tendency has several liabilities: 1) it does not prepare learners for their future; 2) it limits the range of content and teaching methods that can be implemented; 3) it restricts learners' ability to express knowledge about content (assessment); and, most importantly, 4) it constricts the kinds of learners who can be successful.

Checkpoint *5.2: Use multiple tools for construction and composition* asks teachers to provide students with different ways of constructing and creating. The exclusive use of text-based formats will not meet the needs of the variety of learners in our classrooms. Some of our students will need other formats, including high-tech, low-tech, and no-tech options, in order to remove barriers that stand in the way of them creating and composing in a way that authentically represents their skills and passions.

BUILD FLUENCIES WITH GRADUATED LEVELS OF SUPPORT FOR PRACTICE AND PERFORMANCE (5.3)

Research papers have never been my friends. Through my entire undergraduate coursework, I felt like my professors just expected me to know a) what the heck a "research paper" was, b) how to find information, c) how to construct a research paper, d) what all the components and requirements of a research paper were, and e) how to do all these things in a structured way. I didn't know any of these things. *Imposter syndrome*, the idea that everyone else around me knew what they were doing and I didn't (thus making me an imposter), and fear prevented me from asking someone to clarify these things for me. So, I just fumbled my way through several research papers and ended up with average grades, still not having acquired the skills to draft an effective research paper.

That all changed when, in the coursework for my master's degree, I had to take a research methods course. This one thing, writing research papers, which had typically only accounted for a percentage of my grade, would now be the whole grade for this class. I felt doomed to fail and entered the first class meeting with a sense of dread. Little did I know that this class would change the trajectory of my career and remove my fear of writing. You see, the professor (whose name I can't recall) broke down the entire research paper process into small, manageable chunks and carefully walked us through each step, teaching us all the stuff she wished someone had taught her when she started her graduate school work. I ended the semester with an A, and a paper I'm still proud of today, but more importantly, I suddenly had the sense that if I ever wanted to attempt to get a doctorate degree, I might actually be able to do it! This one thing, writing a research paper, had been the barrier that had prevented me from believing I could be successful in an advanced degree program. And this one teacher, who scaffolded the process and made the implicit parts explicit, turned that completely around for me. This checkpoint, *5.3: Build fluencies with graduated levels of support for practice and performance*, asks teachers to find ways to break the giant boulders in education (for me, research papers) into the pebbles (or smaller chunks) that can make students more successful in meeting their learning goals.

Executive Functions (6)

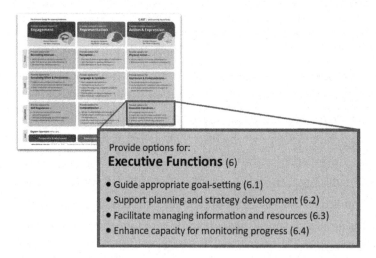

Provide options for:
Executive Functions (6)

- Guide appropriate goal-setting (6.1)
- Support planning and strategy development (6.2)
- Facilitate managing information and resources (6.3)
- Enhance capacity for monitoring progress (6.4)

NOTE: In the world of UDL, the term Executive Functions refers to skills related to organization, planning, and goal-oriented behaviors. No one is born with executive functioning skills, but nearly everyone can learn them! This is great news for students and teachers alike because teachers have the power to be able to help students acquire and strengthen these skills through proactive design using the UDL framework.

GUIDE APPROPRIATE GOAL-SETTING (6.1)

As an ADHD mother of two teenagers who is finishing up a doctoral program while also working full-time, I'm really busy! Most of the time, I'm able to handle the many tasks I must accomplish in a week or a weekend, but occasionally, I have moments when I feel completely overwhelmed. Luckily, my husband, who I've been married to for 20 years (at the writing of this book), knows how my mind works. So, when I get into that mind-space where I can't prioritize what to do next, he often says, "Why don't you make a list?" I usually reply to this with "Why don't *you* make a list?" with all the snark and attitude of a teenaged girl. After 20 years, he smiles and says, "Okay. I'm sure you'll figure something out." Then, of course, when he's out of the room, I promptly make a list and start working through items, one at a time. Soon, I find I've accomplished everything on the list, and I'm able to relax.

What my husband knows, and what I tend to forget when I'm overwhelmed, is that our brains are hardwired to be goal oriented. So, the act of making a list helps me to think through all the mini-goals I need to accomplish and put them down on paper. Sometimes I look at my list and determine that there are way too many items, and I have to prioritize them, saving some things for later. Other times, listing the items helps me realize that I don't have as much to accomplish as I originally thought.

This checkpoint, *6.1: Guide appropriate goal-setting*, reminds teachers that these planning and prioritizing strategies don't come naturally to all students, and that we, as teachers, can help support students' development of these executive function skills by making goal setting part of our regular classroom structure.

SUPPORT PLANNING AND STRATEGY DEVELOPMENT (6.2)

Many students have difficulties planning and prioritizing their study time. Educators can help support these still-developing skills by giving them the tools and strategies they may need to become stronger at organization and time management. This checkpoint, *6.2: Support planning and strategy development*, helps students strengthen these skills by asking the educator to model and scaffold the organization, prioritization, and time-management processes in their classroom.

FACILITATE MANAGING INFORMATION AND RESOURCES (6.3)

When I was a classroom teacher, there was a daily game I'd play with the students in my first-period class. This wasn't a game I wanted to have to play, but it was necessary nonetheless. This game was called "Find Mrs. P's Coffee." You see, when I taught art lessons, I was constantly circulating the room, helping individual students and refilling materials. Inevitably, I would set my coffee cup down somewhere and walk away without even a thought. When I realized I had misplaced my coffee, we would start an exciting game of "Find Mrs. P's Coffee," and the student who found my coffee first won a piece of hard candy. Seriously, this was almost every day. Luckily, I was teaching at a school for students with specific learning disabilities, where most students struggled with executive functions, so they completely understood how their adult teacher with ADHD could misplace her coffee on a daily basis. Plus, I was able to use it as a teachable moment!

What I really needed help with was a way to manage my resources (in this case, the indispensable resource of my morning coffee). This checkpoint, *6.3: Facilitate managing information and resources*, asks teachers to help students develop strategies and methods for managing their own stuff. This skill, like most executive functions, isn't really something we're all born with. Organization is a skill that is learned, and some students have an easier time learning organization than others. Teachers can support those students who struggle with organization by providing them with strategies for organization and by consistently checking back in with students' newly learned organizational skills until they have become habitual. We can also support students' organization of information and resources by removing the clutter from things like syllabi, course pages, homework assignments, and communications like emails and newsletters.

ENHANCE CAPACITY FOR MONITORING PROGRESS (6.4)

One of the most common complaints I hear from K–12 students about their teachers is that it takes them *so* long to grade and return work. To be fair, part of the reason for this complaint is that some students tend to be rather impatient. However, when you ask students to clarify why this upsets them so much, their answer is typically something like this:

> Sometimes we don't get graded quizzes and homework back from the teacher until after the test. How am I supposed to know what I need to study for the test if I haven't gotten feedback from the rest of the unit in time?

Now, before you hit "send" on the angry email you just wrote me, let me say that I totally understand how difficult it is to grade and return work in a timely manner. Especially if you are providing rich feedback! The point

I'm trying to make is that in asking for a faster return of graded work, what students may really be saying is that they want to be able to monitor their own progress.

This checkpoint, *6.4: Enhance capacity for monitoring progress*, encourages educators to begin shifting the onus of tracking progress from the external (teacher-monitored progress) to the internal (student-monitored progress). Please note that the checkpoint doesn't ask us to just turn the whole process over to students immediately, but rather, it asks us to enhance the students' capacity for monitoring their own progress through whatever means we have available to us.

Keep Moving Forward

UDL is a journey with many routes. This process is about progress, not perfection. So, wherever you are in your process, keep moving forward, and you're destined to keep making progress!

Part 3

A Collection of UDL-Aligned Strategies

As was mentioned earlier, there is no such thing as a UDL strategy. The UDL framework tells us *what* we can do in our classrooms and instruction to support the learning brain, but *how* we do it is totally up to us! The strategies in this part are merely ideas to help you get your mind thinking of ways to take the actions suggested by the UDL framework. These strategies and ideas have been organized by UDL Guidelines and checkpoints. You can find additional, expanded strategies (some with printables!) on the *tinyurl.com/TransformWithUDL* website.

The strategies that follow are really just examples of ways you *could* carry out the suggestions made by the UDL checkpoints. For example, checkpoint 3.2 tells us that in order to support students' comprehension we may want to try highlighting patterns, critical features, big ideas, and relationships. One way you could do that is by using a concept map. But can you think of other ways you could help students pull out the big themes or concepts from the content? I'm sure you already have some ideas. Use these strategies to help clarify your understanding of the checkpoints within the UDL framework and to act as a starting point for your own unique ideas!

Principle 1: Engagement

• •

Strategies to Recruit Interest to Improve/ Deepen Motivation

- ▶ Recruiting Interest
    - ▶ 7.1: Optimize individual choice and autonomy
    - ▶ 7.2: Optimize relevance, value, and authenticity
    - ▶ 7.3: Minimize threats and distractions
- ▶ Sustaining Effort & Persistence
    - ▶ 8.1: Heighten salience of goals and objectives
    - ▶ 8.2: Vary demands and resources to optimize challenge
    - ▶ 8.3: Foster collaboration and community
    - ▶ 8.4: Increase mastery-oriented feedback
- ▶ Self Regulation
    - ▶ 9.1: Promote expectations and beliefs that optimize motivation
    - ▶ 9.2: Facilitate personal coping strategies
    - ▶ 9.3: Develop self-assessment and reflection

Recruiting Interest (7)

Optimize individual choice and autonomy (7.1)

★ **Choice of Tools:** Allow students to choose what medium they want to work in (on paper, on the computer, on a whiteboard, etc.), what tools they want to use (manipulatives, pencils, gel pens, etc.), and what aids they might need (a thesaurus, a calculator, etc.).

★ **Choice of Supports:** Allow students to choose whichever supports they need to be successful with the given task: graphic organizers, checklists, templates, examples, anchor charts, strategies, and so on. Provide these supports for all students instead of only students with IEPs.

★ **Tic-Tac-Toe Assignments: Offering Choice of Assessment Type:** Although it's not always possible to offer a choice of assessment type (for example, in a writing class, you have to write), this strategy can be beneficial when teachers are looking to increase engagement and assignment completion rate. The Tic-Tac-Toe strategy allows students to choose three different activities in order to form a tic-tac-toe (three in a row), but teachers strategically place more rigorous options in specific locations to ensure that no student just picks all the easy options. For more information on Tic-Tac-Toe assignments, visit the *tinyurl.com/TransformWithUDL* website.

Optimize relevance, value, and authenticity (7.2)

★ **"So That I Can" Statements:** All too often educators are indirectly asking students to do the work "because they said so." Students typically don't respond well to readings, assignments, and activities they find to be irrelevant. Although many teachers understand the reasoning behind the work they ask students to do, they often fail to make this connection clear to students. A good first step is to phrase all learning targets and student learning outcomes from the student perspective. Sometimes these are referred to as "I Can" statements. When we start our learning objectives with an I Can statement, we are causing ourselves to critically consider what the lesson or activity is really about. Once your learning objective is set in an I Can statement, it helps to clarify your reasoning for choosing that particular lesson or activity. One interesting way I've seen teachers accomplish this is by following up all learning targets and student learning objectives with a section that extends the learning target with the phrase, "So that I can ..." For example, an AP Earth Sciences teacher might post the following learning target on their board to inform students about what they will be doing that day in class:

EXAMPLE OF A LEARNING TARGET

Learning Target 2/28:

I can use objects found around the classroom to make a model of the three types of tectonic plate boundaries.

EXAMPLE OF A LEARNING TARGET WITH A "SO THAT I CAN" STATEMENT

Learning Target 2/28:

I can use objects found around the classroom to make a model of the three types of tectonic plate boundaries *so that I can* have a better understanding of the ways that tectonic plate interactions affect geologic features.

★ **Student Interest Inventory:** In order to know what is relevant to our students, we have to spend some time getting to know them. One simple way to do this is to have students complete a simple student interest inventory at the beginning of the school year or semester.

There are tons of examples of student interest inventories online, but students can write an easy version on an index card when you ask them to add their name and list the following information:

★ **Three things** they care about

★ **Two things** they are good at

★ **One thing** they want their teacher to know about how they learn

Ideally, you will use this information throughout the year to help students brainstorm ideas for topics, projects, and assignments that will be relevant to them.

★ **Make a Meme:** One fun way to make content relevant to students is by asking them to use current media formats to make analogies to what they are learning about. For details on how to use this idea in your classroom, see *Make a Meme* on the *tinyurl.com/TransformWithUDL* website.

Minimize threats and distractions (7.3)

★ **Totes McGoats:** Place plastic totes, baskets, or storage bins that contain commonly needed materials like sharpened pencils, sticky notes, and highlighters strategically around the room for quick student access. The fewer loud pencil sharpeners grinding away during your explanation of directions, the better able your students will be to focus and comprehend.

★ **Low-Risk and No-Risk Assignments:** Consider the option of giving students versions of assignments that are not tied to grades but that will benefit them in the long run. For example, if part of a larger project is turning in a list of references or works cited early in the process, consider giving a completion grade, as opposed to a grade based on how accurately they have used the correct formatting. It can be helpful to consider what the goal is for that part of the assignment and base your grading solely on that factor. So, if the goal of having students turn in references early in the process is to make sure they are able to locate good resources and to make sure they stay on track to finish the assignment, it doesn't make sense to grade their understanding and use of a specific citation format.

★ **Distract at the Back:** Consider the layout of your room in relation to where the most activity will take place. For example, instead of putting frequently used items like tissues, the trash can, sanitizer, and the pencil sharpener at the front of the classroom, consider moving these to the back. That way, students' attention doesn't get pulled away by watching their classmates walk between their seats and the teacher.

Sustaining Effort & Persistence (8)

Heighten salience of goals and objectives (8.1)

★ **Student-Designed Rubrics:** When creating rubrics for projects and assignments, have students help. Give students the learning goals or learning outcomes for the assignment and let them brainstorm some criteria that would demonstrate mastery for each of the goals.

★ **Backwards Design:** Backwards design is a way to plan instruction by starting with the goal, then determining the assessment, and finally, planning the learning activities. For directions on how to use backwards design for planning instruction, visit *tinyurl.com/ TransformWithUDL*.

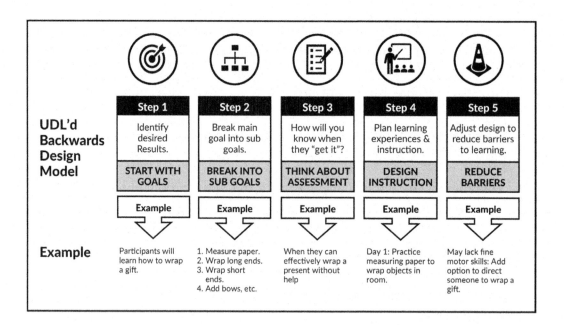

	Step 1	Step 2	Step 3	Step 4	Step 5
UDL'd Backwards Design Model	Identify desired Results.	Break main goal into sub goals.	How will you know when they "get it"?	Plan learning experiences & instruction.	Adjust design to reduce barriers to learning.
	START WITH GOALS	**BREAK INTO SUB GOALS**	**THINK ABOUT ASSESSMENT**	**DESIGN INSTRUCTION**	**REDUCE BARRIERS**
	Example	Example	Example	Example	Example
Example	Participants will learn how to wrap a gift.	1. Measure paper. 2. Wrap long ends. 3. Wrap short ends. 4. Add bows, etc.	When they can effectively wrap a present without help	Day 1: Practice measuring paper to wrap objects in room.	May lack fine motor skills: Add option to direct someone to wrap a gift.

Vary demands and resources to optimize challenge (8.2)

TO VARY RESOURCES

★ **Options for Writing:** Are students fatigued with writing by hand? Let them choose to write or type. Are students struggling with typing (or with spelling or grammar)? Let them choose to type or to use a dictation feature (speech to text).

★ **Flyswatter Flashcards:** Studying vocabulary or spelling can be tedious and even painful for many students and their families. This can be especially true for younger students who may not yet see the value of practicing memory recall. One way to make studying more fun, and to build endurance for longer study periods (i.e., sustaining effort and persistence) is to combine rote-memorization exercises with something fun . . . like hitting stuff with a flyswatter! If students are studying state capitals, for example, add each state on one side of an index card and the corresponding capital on the other. It can be fun to draw a fly on each side of the card too. Start with the state sides facing up, and spread the cards out, all over the table or floor. Give the student a clean, new flyswatter (you can purchase these for a dollar or less at many discount stores). The study partner (who could be a parent, sibling, tutor, fellow student, etc.) then reads a state capital from a list, and the student uses the flyswatter to swat the card with the corresponding state written on it. If they get it right, they get to take that card out of the pile and put it in their "dead fly" pile. If they get it wrong, the card stays on the floor with the rest of the cards. You can switch this up by turning all the cards over so that the capital side is facing up. In this round, the study partner would read the state, and the student would have to swat the capital.

TO VARY DEMANDS

★ **Roll-a-Die:** Let one representative for the class roll a die to determine a quantity for some aspect of an assignment or activity. For example, in math a student could roll a die, then multiply by 2 or 3 to decide how many problems students have to complete for that week's homework. Or, they could determine how many questions they are required to answer independently before being allowed to work together in groups to finish the rest of the questions.

★ **Countdown Timer:** Determine what you think a reasonable amount of time is for students to complete an activity or assignment (let's say 10 minutes). Subtract about 20% of the time (in this case 20% of 10 minutes would be 2 minutes, so we're left with 8 minutes). Then, challenge students to see if they can sufficiently complete the task in that shortened amount of time. It's totally fine if they don't, but for some students, having a time limit increases their focus. The challenge of beating a clock can work wonders! For increased focus, display the countdown timer on the board or screen and give students periodic warnings: 5-minute warning, 2-minute warning, and so on.

★ **Teaching Up:** Teaching up is a strategy in which the teacher plans instruction at the level of the high-achieving students in the room and provides scaffolds and supports to help all students achieve at this level. See *Teaching Up* on the *tinyurl.com/TransformWithUDL* website.

Foster collaboration and community (8.3)

FOSTERING COLLABORATION

★ **Create a "Buddy System":** Have students choose a partner. Then combine one partner pair with another partner pair, forming a group of four. This way each student still has a friend with them, but the teacher can strategically place students in groups as needed.

1. Students choose partners.

2. Teacher combines two (or more) pairs into a group.

★ **Group by Skill:** In this grouping method, students decide which of the predetermined group roles best suits their skills and interests, and then they form a group with one student from each role category.

For more information on the skill-based grouping method, visit the *tinyurl.com/TransformWithUDL* website.

FOSTERING COMMUNITY

★ **Mini Museum of Me:** Toward the beginning of the semester or year, choose one day on which to have students curate a mini museum that displays artifacts that represent themselves. Each student could have a desktop, half of a tabletop, or a whole table (depending on the available space and the number of students) where they could curate a mini museum exhibit about themselves. They may include photos, favorite books, favorite music artists, family mementos, trophies, and anything else they are proud of or want to share about themselves. Once all students have displayed their mini museums, give them ample time to visit and look at each other's displays. Giving students the opportunity to show who they are can be a powerful moment of community building in a classroom, and doing so will give you enormous insight into your students' background, experiences, interests, and talents. (I first learned this strategy of creating mini museums from a friend and colleague, Dr. James-Etta, an expert in culturally responsive teaching. Learn more about her work at *DrJamesEtta.com*.)

Increase mastery-oriented feedback (8.4)

★ **Around-the-World Peer Feedback: Group Rounds:** When asking students to provide peer feedback for written work, give them a structure that allows them to have their work reviewed in four different rounds with each round focusing on one aspect of the paper. Divide students into groups of three to four, and have each group sit in a circle. Students begin by passing their paper to the person on their right. After each round, they pass the paper in their hands to the person on their right. This works best if students are provided with the final grading rubric. For each round, the entire group is reviewing one aspect of the paper they are holding by writing comments on sticky notes and placing the sticky notes on the paper. Each round corresponds to a different element of the rubric:

1. **Content:** Does the paper have all the things it's supposed to have?

2. **Examples and citations:** Have they cited things correctly? Do the examples make sense?

3. **Language and grammar:** Are the language and grammar in line with the rubric?

4. **Overall structure and flow:** Thinking of the piece as a whole, does the structure make sense? Does the paper have effective transitions between sections?

★ **Multiple-Choice Test Corrections:** Some teachers like to offer students the opportunity to correct their tests for partial credit. This works for some assessment types, but what about multiple-choice questions? If they just change their original answer, B, to the correct answer, C, is that really helping them master content? Probably not. Instead, in order to obtain partial credit for test corrections, teachers can ask students to craft a sentence explaining *why* C is the right answer and a sentence for each of the other answers explaining *why* it is wrong.

Self Regulation (9)

Promote expectations and beliefs that optimize motivation (9.1)

★ **Examples, Examples, Examples:** One very simple way to be explicit in our expectations for students is to provide examples. Giving students an example will help you clarify the things you've indicated in your rubric or assignment (length, requirements, etc.) and will also help clarify things you may have forgotten to mention (voice, audience, type of academic language, etc.). Don't have any good student examples? Create your own! Making your own examples for students also helps you to see where some of the barriers might occur for students. This information could be used to help you address these issues in future classes proactively.

★ **Checklist Rubrics—Explicit Expectations:** Many rubrics include category descriptors that are vague, like "Neatness" and "Language Usage." Although the educator knows what to expect for each of these categories, the student probably doesn't. One way to clarify these expectations is to think of three main things (criteria) you might be looking for in that category, then set up your point columns according to how many of these three criteria the student met. (See *Checklist Rubrics* on the *tinyurl.com/TransformWithUDL* website).

Facilitate personal coping skills and strategies (9.2)

★ **Restart Signals:** Some students seem to ask to use the bathroom, or get a drink of water, *every single day*. This can often feel disruptive and disrespectful to the teacher. But in many cases, what these students are actually asking for is a restart. They may be able to sit passively for 10–15 minutes, but after this, they realize that they have become restless, and unless something changes, they may start to become disruptive. So, instead of distracting their neighbors, they ask to go to the bathroom or get a drink. This quick change of scenery serves as a restart button, allowing them to restart their internal sitting-still clock. Although it may seem like this need for a restart only applies to younger students, it most definitely also applies to older K–12 students and even college students. In order to avoid students disrupting the class flow by asking to use the bathroom, you can prearrange a signal that students can use when they need a restart. This signal lets you, the teacher, know that the student is not being rude but rather recognizes that they need to restart their internal sitting-still clock.

To set this up at the beginning of the school year or semester, explain the concepts of needing a restart and the internal sitting-still clock to your students. Then, tell them that you are okay with them getting up and running out for a quick restart, but you would appreciate it if they let you know in an unobtrusive (or distraction-free) way. Some teachers will have students simply hold up the American Sign Language (ASL) sign for the letter R (for "restart") and wait for the teacher to nod in acknowledgment.

★ **Built-in Breaks:** One of my favorite best practices is posting an agenda for each class meeting because it gives students a preview of the learning objectives and activities for that class period. Depending on the length of your class, it can be helpful to build one or more 5-minute breaks into your agenda. This allows students to build self-regulation skills so they can wait for the built-in break that is coming up soon instead of leaving to run to the restroom in the middle of important portions of content delivery.

★ **Checklists:** In his 2009 bestseller, *The Checklist Manifesto*, author Atul Gawande explains that something as simple as a well-constructed checklist has the potential to protect against simple errors. Instead of handing students a wall-of-text version of directions or instructions for an assignment, consider making these into a checklist. In most word processing programs, like Microsoft Word or Google Docs, it is easy to use the bullet point feature for this task. However, instead of using the traditional circle for a bullet point, you can define your own new bullet point; you can choose a hollow square or rectangle, which are typically found in the symbols part of word processing programs.

Develop self-assessment and reflection (9.3)

★ **Metacognitive Moments:** The first time I heard about the concept of *metacognition* (thinking about one's own thinking) was when I was taking classes for my master's degree in teaching. How is it possible that I got through my entire K–12 and undergrad (taking many courses in education) without being asked to consider how I learn best? When I took the time to actually assess my own learning, I had an immediate improvement in learning, retention, and grades. Metacognitive activities can have a profound effect on our students, but we may have to initiate this internal conversation for them. Teachers can build in small moments throughout their class that ask students questions like: How did you study for this exam? How did that work for you? What was easiest for you to remember? What parts were consistently difficult to remember? A quick internet search for *metacognition* and *classroom activities* will turn up many great ideas for building metacognitive activities into your instruction.

★ **Built-in Reflections:** Asking students to reflect on what they just learned is another great way to help them develop self-assessment. Like metacognition, reflection asks students to step back and take an outside look at their own learning, but whereas metacognitive activities are not necessarily an everyday strategy, reflections *can* be built into every class meeting. Over the previous two decades, exit slips have become a common practice used in many K–12 and postsecondary classrooms. I've seen a shift from exit slips being used as reflective tools to exit slips being used as assessment tools, however. Although this is certainly an acceptable practice in some scenarios, teachers should consider building in no-stakes (ungraded) reflections throughout the class period. Ask students to reflect on their mood using a mood meter; ask students to reflect on what was just taught (what made sense and what didn't); and ask students to reflect on things like their choice of group partners or their choice of seating. Regularly asking students to reflect will model the practices of expert learners, and soon they'll be reflecting on their own without being prompted.

★ **Self-Monitoring:** Self-monitoring, like many other forms of self-regulation, is not a skill that humans are born with; it must be learned. You may be asking yourself, "Right, I get that. But what if students arrive in my class without having learned how to monitor their own behavior?" Well, there's good news . . . you're not too late! Self-monitoring can be taught—even to middle schoolers, high schoolers, and college students. One such strategy makes self-monitoring explicit by using a chart and reward system to visually show students how the behavioral choices they are using in the classroom are impacting them and others. For more information on the strategy of *Self-Monitoring,* visit the *tinyurl.com/TransformWithUDL* website.

Principle 2:
Representation

● ●

Strategies to Improve Student Understanding and Retention

- ▶ Perception

    - ▶ 1.1: Offer ways of customizing the display of information

    - ▶ 1.2: Offer alternatives for auditory information

    - ▶ 1.3: Offer alternatives for visual information

- ▶ Language & Symbols

    - ▶ 2.1: Clarify vocabulary and symbols

    - ▶ 2.2: Clarify syntax and structure

    - ▶ 2.3: Support decoding of text, mathematical notation, and symbols

    - ▶ 2.4: Promote understanding across languages

    - ▶ 2.5: Illustrate through multiple media

- ▶ Comprehension

    - ▶ 3.1: Activate or supply background knowledge

    - ▶ 3.2: Highlight patterns, critical features, big ideas, and relationships

    - ▶ 3.3: Guide information processing and visualization

    - ▶ 3.4: Maximize transfer and generalization

Perception (1)

Offer ways of customizing the display of information (1.1)

★ **Include Digital Versions of Documents:** Provide students with digital versions of any documents that you will hand out in paper form. Most devices are capable of zooming in and out and adjusting the brightness, and some can even change the contrast between the text and the background. So, rather than printing out multiple sizes of the same document, educators can simply provide the digital version and allow students to adjust the size, brightness, and contrast to meet their needs.

★ **Use Built-in Heading Styles in Microsoft Word and Google Docs:** If I were creating a document for fully sighted students, I might use a larger font or bolded text to show the difference between the title, the section headings, and the main text. However, for students who use a screen reader, these visual differences are all read the same by the program unless the person creating the document has intentionally made it accessible. In order to set up a more accessible document for student use, use the preset styles in your word processing program (like Microsoft Word or Google Docs). These styles are already set up to tell screen-reader users the kind of text being read, which makes the document much clearer and easier to navigate for students using this assistive technology.

★ **Provide Accessibility Features:** Most smartphones, and some tablets, are equipped with accessibility features that can help students customize the display of information by touching their screen. In addition to allowing users to manipulate the size, brightness, and contrast of text, many of these devices have their own screen-reader feature that can be set up to read the text on the screen aloud. Most personal devices have the capability to dictate the spoken word and turn it into text on the screen. It is vital not only that we provide these accessibility features to our students but that we help them learn how and when to use them.

Offer alternatives for auditory information (1.2)

★ *See* **It Once,** *Say* **It Once:** How many times do teachers give directions only to have students repeatedly ask questions like, "Wait. What are we supposed to do?" If teachers don't want to repeat directions over and over again, they can present them auditorily as well as visually. If students can *see* written directions once, teachers will only have to *say* them once. Try it yourself! Give only spoken directions, then count how many times students ask you to repeat or clarify the directions. Then, later, give spoken directions accompanied by written directions and count how many times students ask you to repeat or clarify.

★ **Captioning Helps Everyone:** Although closed captioning was originally created to assist individuals who could not hear the spoken content, today nearly all of us use captioning in some form or another. In fact, a study by the United Kingdom's Office of Communications (2006) revealed that 80% of people who use closed captioning are not deaf or hearing impaired! I can only assume this number has increased with the popularity of smartphone technology. Captions can also have major implications on education, as was shown in a 2015 meta-analysis by Morton Ann Gernsbacher, which shows that captions can aid with recall and memory retention. So, if you are showing a video in class, consider turning on the captions!

★ **Use Familiar Objects:** Complex concepts can often be clarified by representing them with objects familiar to students. For example, to represent the gravitational pull of the sun, a science teacher might place a bowling ball in the middle of a trampoline and then add marbles that would display the orbit of the planets and how they're kept in orbit. Giving students a visual, tactile, or kinesthetic representation of complex concepts like this can aid in understanding and promote memory retention.

Offer alternatives for visual information (1.3)

★ **Audiobook Versions:** More and more publishers are providing audiobook versions of their texts, and teachers can search online for audiobook versions of texts they commonly use in their class. Additionally, many personal devices are capable of reading text aloud, so providing students with a digital form of texts, articles, and books gives them the option of listening to the text.

★ **Dictation Features:** *Dictation features* are speech-to-text tools that translate the spoken word into typed text. If you've ever asked Siri to send a text while you're driving, you've used dictation tools. A student may need to utilize a dictation feature for many different reasons: fine-motor dexterity, poor typing skills, spelling problems, dyslexia, and so on. But some students use dictation tools to better manage their time. For example, I commute about an hour each way to work every day, and I've used the dictation feature on my smartphone to record text for a presentation I'm planning as I drive. I heard a keynote delivered by Jonathan Mooney, author of *Normal Sucks: How to Live, Learn, and Thrive Outside the Lines* and *The Short Bus: A Journey Beyond Normal*, in which he shared that he'd written several of his books by dictating each chapter into his smartphone. According to his web page (*jonathanmooney.com/about*), Mooney is a "dyslexic writer, speaker, and do-gooder who did not learn to read until 12 years old." For him, the dictation tool removed barriers, allowing this high school dropout to become an award-winning author.

Language & Symbols (2)

Clarify vocabulary and symbols (2.1)

★ **Assume Nothing:** Educators often assume that students come into their classroom having already learned a certain level of foundational vocabulary and background information. This reminds me of something my high school drama teacher, Mr. Russell, used to say, "Assuming makes an A** out of U and ME (ASSUME)". So true! When an educator hits the ground running in a lesson, without reviewing prerequisite background knowledge and vocabulary, they may accidentally leave some students behind. This checkpoint suggests that teachers should not assume their students have retained any information or vocabulary they may have learned in previous semesters or school years. Rather, educators should build regular reviews of vocabulary and symbols into their lessons.

★ **Alphabet Soup:** Acronyms are ubiquitous in the field of education. Here's an example:

We need to set a date for an ARC to discuss Marc's IEP. His recent diagnoses of an SLD and ADHD may have knocked him out of the first two levels of RTI. Please let me know, ASAP, when we can meet!

If you can read this sentence, you might be a special educator. If you are completely confused, you are not alone!

Here's the translation:

We need to set a date for an Admissions and Release Committee (ARC) meeting to discuss Marc's Individualized Education Plan (IEP). His recent diagnoses of a Specific Learning Disability (SLD) and Attention-Deficit Hyperactivity Disorder (ADHD) may have knocked him out of the first two levels of Response to Intervention (RTI). Please let me know, as soon as possible (ASAP) when we can meet!

When we use acronyms and jargon, we can make the processing and retention of information very difficult for those who are unfamiliar with or may have forgotten the meanings of these words and abbreviations. Anytime you use an acronym, regardless of whether you are talking to students, families, administrators, conference participants, or fellow teachers, be sure to use the long form at least once in order to clarify your meaning.

Clarify syntax and structure (2.2)

★ **Color-Coding:** When looking at a text, ask students to highlight or circle different pieces using color-coding. For example, a middle school language arts teacher might ask students to read through a complex poem and highlight all positive words in yellow and all negative words in green, which might be used to show the author's vacillation on the topic.

★ **Live Annotation:** One way to model good reading habits is to share a text example and explicitly point out how you go about reading it. Put the example up on the screen and annotate it in real time, while saying out loud the things you are thinking in your head. Highlight significant information, circle things that are important, and add notes in the margins. These are things that expert readers do, but novice readers often need to be shown how to process the texts they are reading. K–8 teachers can model skills like making inferences and asking questions about the author's intent or use of figurative language, while making annotations on the screen or board for students to see.

Support decoding of text, mathematical notation, and symbols (2.3)

★ **Audible Graphing Calculator:** How do students with visual impairments use a graphing calculator? Well, there's an online graphing calculator called Desmos that interacts with a student's screen reader and represents graphs through the use of sounds, intervals, and tones. For a quick demonstration of the accessibility features of the Desmos calculator, visit *desmos.com/accessibility*.

★ **Cookie Sheet Spelling:** When learning to spell, younger students who struggle with fine-motor skills, writing, and reading may encounter barriers when practicing spelling with a pencil and paper. You can remove these barriers by creating a classroom set of tactile language arts manipulatives with cookie sheets and magnetic letters from your local dollar store. These cookie sheet spelling manipulatives also stack neatly for easy and compact storage! World language teachers can use cookie sheet spelling to practice spelling or word recognition with older students by giving them the non-English word and then having them spell out the English word with magnet letters and hold up their own individual cookie sheet—in the same way one might use a whiteboard.

Promote understanding across languages (2.4)

★ **Nonlinguistic Supports:** When designing worksheets, posters, handouts, slides, and other instructional materials, add visual supports that help to convey understanding. Images, icons, videos, graphs, and diagrams help English learners clarify the text-based information in the classroom.

★ **Auto-Caption Slides Presentations:** Google Slides and the Office 365 version of PowerPoint both offer the option of auto-captioning the speaker during live slide presentations. Turn this feature on during your live lectures or slide presentations to support all students, including students who are English learners, students with auditory processing barriers, and students who struggle with maintaining focus and attention.

★ **Provide Slides Before Class:** One very simple way to support students' understanding of content delivered via slide presentation is to send out a link to the slides before class. This will benefit all students but will be especially helpful to students who may need to use translation software ahead of time, students who have fine-motor impairments, and students who struggle with short-term memory and processing.

Illustrate through multiple media (2.5)

★ **The Fortune Teller Partner Quiz (FTPQ)** strategy gives students a chance to make it, act on it, read it, see it, and hear it, while it also gives them the opportunity to review content by moving around the room and interacting with their classmates. When students are provided with multiple means of representation, they are much more likely to retain the content. For more information on the FTPQ strategy, visit *tinyurl.com/TransformWithUDL*.

★ **Book and Look:** When you ask students to read a text, add a visual (graphic or diagram) to clarify complex sections or concepts.

★ **Manipulate and Make:** Manipulatives are not just for math anymore! Can you find a way for students to get their hands on some part of the content? Use everyday objects to make a connection to what you are teaching. Use a metal spring to demonstrate how sound waves travel. Or use self-hardening chocolate sauce poured over a scoop of ice cream to show how an exoskeleton protects the bodies of insects and crustaceans. You can even have students go through the process of mummification by cutting open a small plush toy, removing its organs (stuffing) and storing them in a canopic jar, sewing the toy up, and mummifying it. Using manipulatives and making objects is a great way to give some of our more active learners another on-ramp to the content.

★ **Simulations:** One way to get students actively involved in learning is to use simulations. Simulations are used for training in many fields, including aviation and medicine, and can have a similar effect when used in the classroom. Students can feel what it's like in a certain experiential setting without needing safety equipment, paramedics, or time travel. While many digital simulations are online, other forms, like historical simulations and medical simulations, can often be carried out in the classroom setting. Of course, you always need to consider the ethical and emotional concerns surrounding historical simulations through the perspective of your students. Simulating or re-creating traumatic experiences can be harmful to students and should be avoided. For one perspective on using historical simulations in the classroom, check out *Cult of Pedagogy* blogger Jennifer Gonzalez's interview with Hasan Kwame Jeffries at *https://www.cultofpedagogy.com/classroom-simulations/*.

Comprehension (3)

Activate or supply background knowledge (3.1)

★ **Snowball Fight:** A snowball fight is an active review strategy in which students answer a review prompt on a sticky note (or slip of paper); then they each crumble up their paper into a tiny ball and throw the snowballs back and forth until the teacher tells them to stop. When they stop, they quickly find a snowball (plenty will be on the floor, under desks, and on tables), form groups of three to five, and discuss the answers written in the snowballs they are holding. For more information on the Snowball Fight activity, visit the *tinyurl.com/TransformWithUDL* website.

★ **Swap Meet/Yes, and . . . :** This activity gets learners up and out of their seats in a content review activity that takes what they know about a subject and adds to it using a "Yes, and . . ." activity. For more information on the Swap Meet/Yes, and . . . activity, visit the *tinyurl.com/TransformWithUDL* website.

★ **Background Knowledge Video:** This strategy asks educators to make a short, simple review video that brings all students up to speed on prerequisite knowledge before starting a new unit or module. This video can be assigned as homework or played during class.

Highlight patterns, critical features, big ideas, and relationships (3.2)

★ **Card Sorting:** In a card-sorting activity, students sort prepared cards (index cards work well) into categories based on given criteria. This hands-on activity helps students physically categorize content that can aid in comprehension and retention.

★ **Hula-Hoop Venn Diagram:** When comparing and contrasting two (or three) items, add characteristics or traits to individual index cards, then lay hula hoops on the ground in the shape of a Venn diagram. Have students physically place the cards in the appropriate place within the diagram. Have students pose for a photo with their diagram and use the photo to check for understanding.

★ **Text Feature Tour: Headers and Subheaders:** Before beginning a chapter, walk students through it by making an outline of its headings and subheadings on the board or screen. This helps them to see the main points, and the subpoints that fit under them as well.

Guide information processing and visualization (3.3)

★ **Mnemonic Devices:** A mnemonic device is a strategy used to help with memory and information processing. Mnemonic devices can be used to group information for easy memorization. One example is using PEMDAS to remember the order of operations used in solving algebraic math problems:

P= Parentheses

E= Exponents

M= Multiplication

D= Division

A= Addition

S= Subtraction

Help students group and remember information by creating a mnemonic device to accompany new information.

★ **Graphic Organizers:** A graphic organizer is a simple way to graphically (or visually) organize information. A Venn diagram is a simple example of a graphic organizer, and a basic table can be used to help categorize or classify information in a visual format. Find a graphic organizer online or make your own using a drawing or desktop publishing program, or simply draw one and make copies. Graphic organizers will help students make connections between concepts by allowing them to see the visual connection on the page and will aid in the processing of information.

★ **Character Yearbook** (fiction): When reading a novel, some students will become confused about which character is which. Ameliorate this problem by creating a one-page character yearbook. On this page, you list the character's name, important relationships, and a brief description of that character's traits. If you have any strong artists in your class, have them make an image of each character based on that character's description in the book. Give each student a copy of the character yearbook to refer to as they read through the book.

★ **Roll-a-Chapter:** The Roll-a-Chapter activity is a fun alternative to a reading guide that allows students to demonstrate their understanding of characters and events within a chapter in several different ways. Students roll a die to determine which questions to answer first, second, and so on. For more information, including reproducible templates, visit the *tinyurl.com/TransformWithUDL* website.

Maximize transfer and generalization (3.4)

★ **Embed Study Skills:** Teachers can build study skills into their classes by making them part of a grade. For example, teach students how to improve their scores on multiple-choice tests by making 5 points count for students underlining key words, circling transition words, and crossing out obviously wrong answers. So, 95 of the points for the test would be from the actual test answers, and 5 of the points would be for using test-taking strategies.

★ **Cubing:** Cubing is a way to look at a concept from all angles at the same time. This is similar to the idea of Cubism in art: Picasso's unique style is defined by his concept of depicting one object or figure from many angles at the same time. For more information on Cubing, visit the *tinyurl.com/TransformWithUDL* website.

Principle 3:
Action & Expression

· ·

Strategies to Guide and Enhance Learning and Retention

- ▶ Physical Action
  - ▶ 4.1: Vary the methods for response and navigation
  - ▶ 4.2: Optimize access to tools and assistive technologies
- ▶ Expression & Communication
  - ▶ 5.1: Use multiple media for communication
  - ▶ 5.2: Use multiple tools for construction and composition
  - ▶ 5.3: Build fluencies with graduated levels of support for practice and performance
- ▶ Executive Functions
  - ▶ 6.1: Guide appropriate goal setting
  - ▶ 6.2: Support planning and strategy development
  - ▶ 6.3: Facilitate managing information and resources
  - ▶ 6.4: Enhance capacity for monitoring progress

Physical Action (4)

Vary the methods for response and navigation (4.1)

★ **Gallery Walk:** A *Gallery Walk* is an activity that gets students up and out of their seats as they move around the room reading and holding informal discussions at the posters, signs, or papers that have been posted on the walls. For more information on how to use a Gallery Walk in your classroom, visit the *tinyurl.com/TransformWithUDL* website.

★ **Vote With Your Feet:** The Vote With Your Feet (VWYF) strategy is basically a multiple-choice question in real space. The teacher reads a question or an example and students walk to, and stand by, the sign with the correct answer. For more information on the Vote With Your Feet strategy, visit the *tinyurl.com/TransformWithUDL* website.

★ **Back-Channel Google Docs:** A back channel is an informal, anonymous way for students to participate in a lesson, workshop, presentation, or lecture by giving them a space to interact with each other in real time. A simple way to do this is by opening a Google Doc and sharing the link with students. After the live class or session is over, students can refer back to the Google Doc as needed, and the teacher can use the document as an artifact to see areas where there may have been misunderstandings or confusion.

Optimize access to tools and assistive technologies (4.2)

★ **Share Your Slides:** When taking notes, many students are so busy trying to record every word presented on the slides that they miss at least part of the actual spoken content. Providing slides ahead of time reduces the threat of not writing down all the information and allows students to hear more of the content and simply add notes to the text and graphics shown on the slides. Additionally, providing slides ahead of class time is extremely beneficial for students who may struggle with language and text-based formats, such as English language learners, students with specific learning disabilities like dyslexia, and students with attentional barriers like ADHD.

★ **5-Minute Feature:** Some students may not want to use assistive technology because they aren't familiar with the program, tool, or software. Educators could take 5 minutes, once a week, to introduce a tool that may be helpful to students. For example, if students are having trouble keeping up with readings, the teacher can take five minutes to show them how to use the text-to-speech feature on their smartphone or tablet.

Expression & Communication (5)

Use multiple media for communication (5.1)

★ **Silent Conversation:** A silent conversation allows students to have a discussion on paper in small groups, rather than aloud in a whole-class setting. This strategy varies the methods for response and navigation, thus giving students who are reluctant to raise their hands or speak up in class discussions the opportunity to participate in a meaningful way. For more information on how to use the Silent Conversation strategy in your classroom, visit the *tinyurl.com/yourUDL startup* website.

★ **Think-Ink-Pair-Share (T.I.P.S.):** Some educators are familiar with the idea of a Think-Pair-Share, an active learning technique in which educators ask a question, then ask students to 1) *think* about the question, 2) *pair* up with someone else in the room, and 3) *share* their answer with the partner. The Think-Ink-Pair-Share strategy builds in another step in which students take a moment to record their ideas (presumably writing with ink) before sharing them with their partner. For more information on the Think-Ink-Pair-Share strategy, visit the *tinyurl.com/TransformWithUDL* website.

Use multiple tools for construction and composition (5.2)

★ **Sticky-Note Brainstorming:** When they're brainstorming, some students' ideas don't come out in a logical order. It can be helpful for these students to jot down individual ideas on sticky notes first; then once the ideas are all out, they can arrange the sticky notes into a more logical sequence.

★ **Concept Mapping:** A concept map is a visual representation of ideas in which arrows are used to connect concepts on paper.

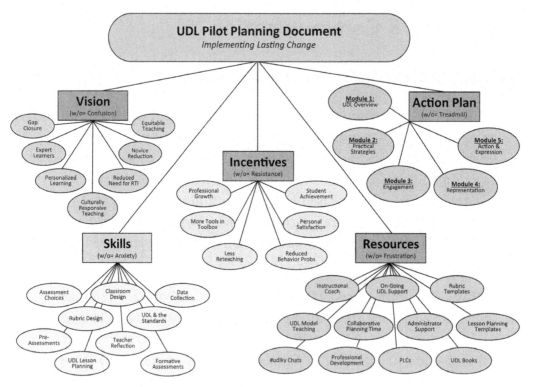

Inspired by Knoster, Villa, & Thousand, 2000

Build fluencies with graduated levels of support for practice and performance (5.3)

★ **I Do, We Do, You Do:** One of my favorite ways to build graduated levels of support is to use modeling in the classroom. The I Do, We Do, You Do strategy consists of a three-part modeling process: 1) I Do—the teacher models the use of the content as students observe; 2) We Do—the students work together in a group to model the same process from Step 1; 3) You Do—having seen the process two times now, students follow the same process individually. Or, more simply,

  ★ **I Do** = teacher models

  ★ **We Do** = students work in groups

  ★ **You Do** = students work individually

Executive Functions (6)

Guide appropriate goal-setting (6.1)

★ **Chunk and Check:** A chapter outline can easily be turned into a checklist for students to "chunk and check." Chunk the chapter by breaking it into smaller sections based on headers and subheaders and check off each section after it is read.

★ **Checklist Directions:** The goal-oriented nature of our brains compels humans to want to check the boxes, so students are more likely to follow multistep directions when they are presented in the form of a checklist. For more information on using checklists, visit the *tinyurl.com/TransformWithUDL* website.

Support planning and strategy development (6.2)

★ **Estimate Homework Time:** When assigning homework, it can be very helpful to provide an estimated homework time so that students can gauge the amount of time required to complete the task. (In fact, many online news sources have begun adding estimated reading times to their articles, presenting readers with a general idea of how much time they are committing to reading the article.) This helps students budget their after-school time while also building time-management skills.

★ **Stoplight Prioritizing:** Some students may really struggle with figuring out where to start on homework, projects, papers, and studying. The Stoplight Prioritizing strategy helps students figure out where to begin by dividing tasks into green light, yellow light, and red light tasks. For more information on the Stoplight Prioritizing strategy, visit *tinyurl.com/TransformWithUDL*.

★ **Give Yourself a Break:** This technique helps students to determine how long they can maintain attention while studying and to build a study and break schedule that will maximize their efficiency and focus over longer periods of time. For more information on the Give Yourself a Break strategy, visit *tinyurl.com/TransformWithUDL*.

Facilitate managing information and resources (6.3)

★ **Clutter-Free Communication:** I've received emails from my daughters' teachers that required multiple page scrolls because of their length. In reality, the things in the email could have been reduced to a few bullet points. If you find that students or families aren't reading the things you're sending out, try limiting your messages to a few bullet points and see if that helps. Obviously, not everything will work in a bullet point list, but even removing one paragraph and replacing it with bullet points will increase the readability of your messages and the likelihood of them actually being read and understood.

Enhance capacity for monitoring progress (6.4)

★ **Think Outside the Box:** I have tried everything I can think of to get my teenage daughter to clean her room. I've set a timer, I've made checklists, I've given rewards, and I've given punishments, but nothing has consistently worked. That is, until she discovered the time-lapse video feature on her phone. For some reason, unbeknownst to me, she is willing to clean her room if she can make a time-lapse video of her room, before, during, and after cleanup, to document her progress. It turns out, my methods of monitoring her progress simply didn't work for her because I hadn't considered that her ideas of progress, and the "how" behind them, may be different than mine. Although we may not be able to submit time-lapse videos for students' IEP progress monitoring (at least not yet), we can take into account students' own ideas of progress. The question is not how will *I* know they've made progress, but rather how will *they* know when they've met their goal?

★ **Board Game Goals:** One fun way to help younger students mark their progress is by using a board game template. You can find many blank board game templates online that would work well for this purpose. Simply set your start as the level where students are now; then, set your end where you'd like to see them within a short timeframe, say four weeks. Next, mark two or three spots along the gameboard path where students can receive a reward when they land there. Finally, let students color or decorate their gameboard.

A Final Word

Before you set this book down, I want to send you off with a quick reflective activity.

1. Set a timer for 3–5 minutes.

2. Skim through your work from the first four steps.

3. When your timer goes off, come back and reflect on the following question:

How has my thinking shifted toward a UDL mindset?

If we keep refining our instruction by searching for and removing barriers, seeking out feedback, and reflecting on our practice, we will be amazed by the changes we see in our classroom. We will have a renewed sense of faith in ourselves and our students. We will not look back on our old teaching as bad, but rather, we will use our experience to inform our future. When we are awakened to the unintentional barriers in our classroom, and when we commit ourselves to designing and reflecting on our instruction to remove these barriers for our students, we're setting up a win-win situation for all involved! Our students will be more engaged, and their self-efficacy will grow as they start to understand how smart and capable they already are. Our own sense of self-efficacy as teachers will grow because we now get to leave our classrooms at the end of the day knowing that we used our design powers to remove learning barriers for our students. We become proud of our practice and we begin to enjoy our students more because we have now situated ourselves as allies and advocates for them, rather than perpetuating old beliefs that may have led us to see students as opponents or enemies.

Does this sound too good to be true? It's not! Teachers all over the globe have seen these benefits materialize as they build UDL into their practice.

For some teachers these benefits may appear quickly, and for others it may take a little more time. But if we keep designing with UDL principles, we too will see amazing changes in ourselves and our students!

> *Remember: Growth may be small and it probably won't be in a straight line.*
>
> The goal is PROGRESS, not PERFECTION.
> Progress is attainable. Perfection is not.

Remember, teaching is called a "practice" for a reason . . . because it takes practice! In fact, in the same way we want our students to become lifelong learners, we, as teachers, want to be lifelong learners in our own teaching practice. Keep looking for growth within yourself and your students, and eventually, you won't believe how far you've come!

I'll leave you with one final thought. I heard this idea many years ago, and it has become part of my own mindset shift. Feel free to make it part of yours, too!

Although I'm not quite where I want to be, I'm so much better off than where I was!

Appendix
CAST UDL Guidelines

The Universal Design for Learning Guidelines

Goal	Internalize	Build	Access	
				Provide multiple means of Engagement
				Affective Networks — The "WHY" of Learning
		Provide options for Recruiting Interest (7)	• Optimize individual choice and autonomy (7.1) • Optimize relevance, value, and authenticity (7.2) • Minimize threats and distractions (7.3)	
	Provide options for Self Regulation (9) • Promote expectations and beliefs that optimize motivation (9.1) • Facilitate personal coping skills and strategies (9.2) • Develop self-assessment and reflection (9.3)	**Provide options for Sustaining Effort & Persistence** (8) • Heighten salience of goals and objectives (8.1) • Vary demands and resources to optimize challenge (8.2) • Foster collaboration and community (8.3) • Increase mastery-oriented feedback (8.4)		
Expert learners who are...				**Provide multiple means of** Representation
				Recognition Networks — The "WHAT" of Learning 
			Provide options for Perception (1) • Offer ways of customizing the display of information (1.1) • Offer alternatives for auditory information (1.2) • Offer alternatives for visual information (1.3)	
	Provide options for Comprehension (3) • Activate or supply background knowledge (3.1) • Highlight patterns, critical features, big ideas, and relationships (3.2) • Guide information processing and visualization (3.3) • Maximize transfer and generalization (3.4)	**Provide options for Language & Symbols** (2) • Clarify vocabulary and symbols (2.1) • Clarify syntax and structure (2.2) • Support decoding of text, mathematical notation, and symbols (2.3) • Promote understanding across languages (2.4) • Illustrate through multiple media (2.5)		
Purposeful & Motivated				**CAST** | Until learning has no limits
Resourceful & Knowledgeable				**Provide multiple means of** Action & Expression
				Strategic Networks — The "HOW" of Learning 
			Provide options for Physical Action (4) • Vary the methods for response and navigation (4.1) • Optimize access to tools and assistive technologies (4.2)	
	Provide options for Executive Functions (6) • Guide appropriate goal-setting (6.1) • Support planning and strategy development (6.2) • Facilitate managing information and resources (6.3) • Enhance capacity for monitoring progress (6.4)	**Provide options for Expression & Communication** (5) • Use multiple media for communication (5.1) • Use multiple tools for construction and composition (5.2) • Build fluencies with graduated levels of support for practice and performance (5.3)		
Strategic & Goal-Directed				

udlguidelines.cast.org | © CAST, Inc. 2018 | Suggested Citation: CAST (2018). Universal design for learning guidelines version 2.2 [graphic organizer]. Wakefield, MA: Author.

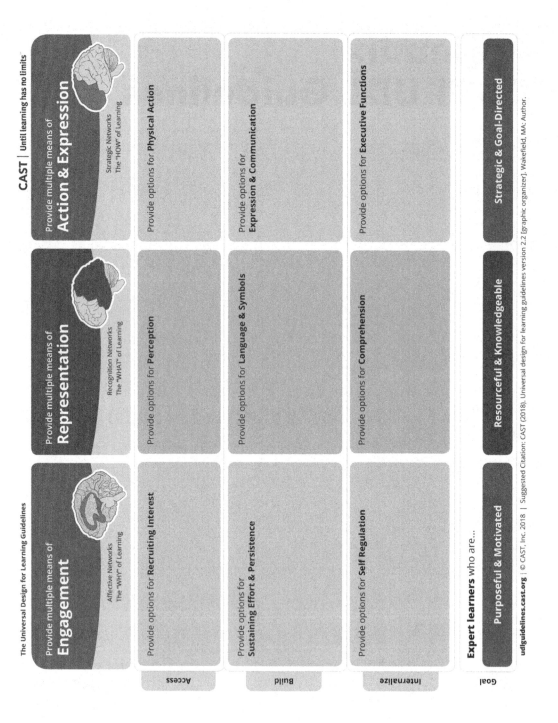

CAST | Until learning has no limits

Provide multiple means of
Engagement

Affective Networks
The "WHY" of Learning

Provide multiple means of
Representation

Recognition Networks
The "WHAT" of Learning

Provide multiple means of
Action & Expression

Strategic Networks
The "HOW" of Learning

Access

Provide options for **Recruiting Interest**

Provide options for **Perception**

Provide options for **Physical Action**

Build

Provide options for
Sustaining Effort & Persistence

Provide options for **Language & Symbols**

Provide options for
Expression & Communication

Internalize

Provide options for **Self Regulation**

Provide options for **Comprehension**

Provide options for **Executive Functions**

Goal

Expert learners who are...

Purposeful & Motivated

Resourceful & Knowledgeable

Strategic & Goal-Directed

udlguidelines.cast.org | © CAST, Inc. 2018 | Suggested Citation: CAST (2018). Universal design for learning guidelines version 2.2 [graphic organizer]. Wakefield, MA: Author.

Bibliography

Brown, P. C., Roediger III, H. L. & McDaniel, M. A. (2014). *Make it stick*. Harvard University Press.

CAST (2018). Universal Design for Learning Guidelines version 2.2. Retrieved from http://udlguidelines.cast.org

Ducharme, K. (2016). Design thinking for educators—Emotion by design. Conference presentation. CAST UDL Symposium, August 9, 2016, Cambridge, MA. Retrieved from https://2016castsymposiuma.sched.com/event/6b53

Gagne, R. M., & Briggs, L. J. (1974). *Principles of instructional design*. Holt, Rinehart & Winston.

Gawande, A. (2009). *The checklist manifesto: How to get things right*. Picador.

Gernsbacher M. A. (2015). Video captions benefit everyone. *Policy Insights From the Behavioral and Brain Sciences, 2*(1), 195–202. Retrieved from https://doi.org/10.1177/2372732215602130

Gonzalez, J. (Host). (2019, July 7). Think Twice Before Doing Another Historical Simulation (No. 125). [Audio podcast episode]. In *Cult of Pedagogy*. Libsyn. https://www.cultofpedagogy.com/classroom-simulations/

Gregory, G. (2013). *Differentiated instructional strategies: One size doesn't fit all*. Corwin Press.

James, W. (1899/2001). *Talks to teachers on psychology and to students on some of life's ideals*. Dover.

Knoster, T., Villa, R. A., and Thousand, J. S. (2000) A framework for thinking about systems change. In R. A. Villa and J. S. Thousand (Eds.) *Restructuring for caring and effective education: Piecing the puzzle together.* (pp. 93–128). Brookes Publishing.

Macan, T. H., Shahani, C., Dipboye, R. L., & Phillips, A. P. (1990). College students' time management: Correlations with academic performance and stress. *Journal of Educational Psychology, 82*(4), 760–768. https://doi.org/10.1037/0022-0663.82.4.760

Meyer, A., Rose, D. H., & Gordon D. (2014). *Universal Design for Learning: Theory and practice.* CAST Professional Publishing.

Nelson, L. L. (2014). *Design and deliver: Planning and teaching using Universal Design for Learning.* Paul H. Brookes Publishing Co.

Novak, K. (2016). *UDL now! A teacher's guide to applying Universal Design for Learning in today's classrooms.* CAST Professional Publishing.

Novak, K. (2022). *UDL now! A teacher's guide to applying Universal Design for Learning* (3rd ed.). CAST Professional Publishing.

Novak, K. & Rodriguez, K. (2018, January). UDL progression rubric. CAST. Retrieved from https://publishing.cast.org/stories-resources/book-product-resources/udl-progression-rubric-novak-rodriguez

Novak, K. & Thibodeau, T. (2016). *UDL in the cloud! How to design and deliver online education using Universal Design for Learning.* CAST Professional Publishing.

Office of Communications. (2006). *Television access services.* Retrieved from https://www.ofcom.org.uk/__data/assets/pdf_file/0016/42442/access.pdf

Posey, A. (2019). *Engage the brain: How to design for learning that taps into the power of emotion.* Association for Supervision and Curriculum Development.

Ralabate, P. K., and Nelson, L. L. (2017). *Culturally responsive design for English learners: The UDL approach.* CAST Professional Publishing.

Rose, D. H. & Meyer, A. (Eds.). (2006). *A practical reader in Universal Design for Learning.* Harvard Education Press.

Schunk, D. H., & Zimmerman, B. J. (1998). *Self-regulated learning: From teaching to self-reflective practice.* Guilford Press.

Tobin, T. J., & Behling, K. T. (2018). *Reach everyone, teach everyone: Universal Design for Learning in higher education.* West Virginia University Press.

Tomlinson, C. A., & Moon, T. R. (2014). *Assessment and student success in a differentiated classroom.* Hawker Brownlow Education.

Vygotsky, L. S. (1978). *Mind in society: The development of higher psychological processes.* Harvard University Press.

Wiggins, Grant P., McTighe, J., Kiernan, L. J., & Frost, F. (1998). *Understanding by design.* Association for Supervision and Curriculum Development.

Index

Page numbers followed by *f* indicate figures.

Acknowledgments

- ★ **To Anne Meyer, David Rose, Grace Meo, and Skip Stahl**, the founders of CAST, for starting the work that would change my life.

- ★ **To CAST and CAST Professional Learning** for selecting me to be part of the CAST National Faculty. I love the work I get to do with CAST Professional Learning! It's so much fun!

- ★ **To David Gordon and CAST Publishing** for removing barriers so I felt comfortable enough to submit a book proposal. Truly, this is *never* something I would have dreamed of had I not sat in your "So you want to write a UDL book"-type session at the 2019 CAST UDL Symposium. Thanks for believing in me and in this work.

- ★ **To Billie Fitzpatrick** for challenging me to take this book to the next level. I'm so glad you were able to help untangle this ADHD brain so that my billions of ideas made sense! Truly—this book wouldn't be what it is today without your patience, advocacy, encouragement, and guidance.

- ★ **To Sister Anne Rita Mauck and Dr. Charles Shedd** who challenged the myth of the average learner in education and removed learning barriers for students with specific learning disabilities at a time when that kind of innovative thinking wasn't the norm in education. The ripples you started in the pond of inclusive education continue to be the waves that carry so many students, families, and teachers toward success.

- ★ **To Tony Kemper, Lisa Stepp, and Phil Howell,** for trusting me to develop dePaul's first arts and humanities program, for believing in my dream of staging a full-scale musical, for believing in the power of the arts in education, and for supporting me at every turn. The teaching experience I gained at dePaul completely changed the trajectory of my life and put me on the path I'm on today. Thank you, from the bottom of my heart.

★ **To the teachers, students, and families of the dePaul School** who opened my eyes to the concept of removing learning barriers and adjusting teaching based on the student needs in the classroom. I am eternally grateful for the experience I gained at this incredible school.

★ **To April Pieper and Amanda Ellis,** who, in my work at the Kentucky Department of Education, asked me to learn about and become a specialist in UDL, sent me to my first CAST UDL Symposium, supported my crazy idea to hold a UDL pilot program, and backed me up every step of the way. You are both incredible leaders with a real passion and a heart for inclusive and equitable teaching, and I appreciate everything you do for students across the Commonwealth of Kentucky.

★ **To Sheri Satterly and Dr. Keith Look**, the principal and superintendent who let me offer the 2017–2018 UDL pilot program in their school. UDL works best in schools where teachers are backed up by their administrators, and your support and encouragement were invaluable to the success of the pilot program. Thank you so much for believing in me!

★ **To all the teachers who participated in the 2017–2018 UDL pilot program** through the Kentucky Department of Education. I learned so much about UDL implementation from heading up this pilot, and that never would have happened without the willingness, flexibility, and passion of Diania, Jessica, Lois, Michelle, Shelby, Stephanie, Susan, and Tressa.

★ **To Lois Sepahban and Shelby Cameron**, the two teacher-leaders who, after participating in the 2017–2018 UDL pilot program, led a summer-long program to introduce UDL to a new cohort of teachers in their school. They invited me to present on UDL lesson planning in this program, which prompted me to think about the three different approaches to UDL lesson planning that serve as the foundation of this book.

★ **To my colleagues at the University of Kentucky's Center for the Enhancement of Learning and Teaching and UK Online** who have expanded my understanding of teaching to include the realm of higher education. Your love of teaching, humor, and camaraderie make my work so rewarding, and I look forward to continuing to "disrupt the norms" in higher ed with you.

★ **To all my "program" friends**, who loved me when I couldn't love myself. Your experience, strength, and hope have given me the confidence, sanity, and serenity I've needed to write this book. Thank you for giving me nearly 14 years in the *sunlight of the spirit*.

★ **To my parents** who are the first and best teachers in my life. Thank you for *literally* everything.

★ **To Joey** who has encouraged this nonwriter to write this book and who has supported me with all the time, love, and space I needed to write it. Thanks for being the best husband and father to my children that I could ever ask for.

★ **To Kira and Sadie,** who show me how to "live, laugh, and love," even when I'm being a "basic white mom" or when I say or do something that is "cringey." I love you so much, and I'm honored that God chose me to be your Mom.

About the Author

Jennifer L. Pusateri

@JEN_PUSATERI (TWITTER)

Photo by Kat's Eye Photography

Jennifer L. Pusateri (pronounced Puu-suh-TEHR-ee) is the Universal Design Consultant for the University of Kentucky's Center for the Enhancement of Learning and Teaching (CELT), where she fosters the advancement of accessibility and inclusive teaching practices across campus. Jennifer also served as a co-leader and charter member of the international UDLHE (UDL in Higher Education) Network.

As a member of the prestigious CAST National Faculty, Jennifer regularly presents UDL workshops and webinars for school districts, college faculty, and state boards of education across the United States. Pusateri has also been featured as a guest UDL specialist in podcasts such as *Think UDL* and *Teaching in Higher Ed*. She also serves as a proud member of her local school board.

Before arriving at the University of Kentucky, Pusateri worked for the Kentucky Department of Education (KDE), where she served as an education consultant and specialist in differentiated learning and Universal Design for Learning (UDL). Jennifer taught Arts and Humanities for grades K–8 at a nationally recognized school for students with specific learning disabilities (SLD) in Louisville, Kentucky.

Jennifer attended the Indiana University School of Music, where she earned her undergraduate degree in vocal music and fine arts. She earned her Master of Arts in Teaching at the University of the Cumberlands and is a PhD candidate in Education Sciences (with a focus on Curriculum and Instruction) at the University of Kentucky. Jennifer currently lives in Central Kentucky with her husband, Joey; her two daughters, Kira and Sadie; her mother, Patti; and her pets, Fiona (dog), and Tasha (cat).